FAMILYLIFE
BIBLE STUDY
FOR COUPLES

Dennis & Barbara Rainey

THOMAS NELSON
Since 1798

NASHVILLE   DALLAS   MEXICO CITY   RIO DE JANEIRO

Published in Nashville, Tennessee, by Thomas Nelson. Thomas Nelson is a trademark of Thomas Nelson, Inc.

Published in association with the literary agency of Wolgemuth & Associates, Inc.

The publisher is grateful to Steve Halliday of Crown Media, Ltd., for his collaboration and writing skills in developing the content for this book from the text of the *FamilyLife Marriage Bible*; notes written by Dennis and Barbara Rainey.

Thomas Nelson, Inc., titles may be purchased in bulk for educational, business, fund-raising, or sales promotional use. For information, please e-mail SpecialMarkets@ThomasNelson.com.

Unless otherwise indicated, scripture quotations are taken from THE NEW KING JAMES VERSION. © 1982 by Thomas Nelson, Inc. Used by permission. All rights reserved.

Scripture quotations marked KJV are taken from the King James Version of the Bible.

Scripture quotations marked NASB are taken from the NEW AMERICAN STANDARD BIBLE®, © The Lockman Foundation 1960, 1962, 1963, 1968, 1971, 1972, 1973, 1975, 1977, 1995. Used by permission.

Scripture quotations marked NIV are taken from the HOLY BIBLE: NEW INTERNATIONAL VERSION®. © 1973, 1978, 1984 by International Bible Society. Used by permission of Zondervan Publishing House. All rights reserved.

Scripture quotations marked RSV are taken from the REVISED STANDARD VERSION of the Bible. © 1946, 1952, 1971, 1973 by the Division of Christian Education of the National Council of the Churches of Christ in the U.S.A. Used by permission.

ISBN: 978-1-4185-4303-7

Printed in the United States of America

HB 08.23.2019

CONTENTS

Introduction. 5

WEEK 1

The Lordship of Christ over All of Life 7

WEEK 2

Marriage as a Covenant Commitment 25

WEEK 3

Successful Marriage-Building Strategies 43

WEEK 4

The Complementary Responsibilities of
    Husbands and Wives. 61

WEEK 5

Living by Faith 75

WEEK 6

Embracing a Sense of Mission 91

WEEK 7

Leaving a Spiritual Legacy 107

Epilogue. 123

Notes. 125

INTRODUCTION

God designed marriage to be the most intimate, fulfilling human relationship this side of heaven. He created the first human couple, Adam and Eve, to reflect His own loving nature and to echo the perfectly harmonious relationship eternally enjoyed by the members of the Trinity.

So what happened? Sin changed everything.

Today, all of us are living out our marriages, not on some romantic balcony, but in the middle of a raging spiritual battlefield. Only through a restored relationship with God through faith in Jesus Christ can you and I begin to enjoy God's original plan and purpose for marriage.

This seven-week study is designed to help married couples of all ages—and at all stages of life—to grow closer to one another as they mature in their relationship with God. Each lesson takes a look at the "big issues" couples face as they work to create a fulfilling life together.

As participants investigate key Bible passages related to marriage and family and explore selected insights from *The FamilyLife Marriage Bible*, they will gain the tools to deepen their marital union and strengthen their families. Each lesson features three main sections:

- Ponder on Your Own

- Discuss with Your Spouse

- Study with Your Group

While the arrangement of these sections may vary slightly from lesson to lesson, each week offers participants an in-depth opportunity to interact with selected Scripture passages in connection with relevant, practical commentary. Thoughtful questions lead participants into a deeper understanding and personal application of God's Word. The seven lessons include:

1. The Lordship of Christ over All of Life

2. Marriage as a Covenant Commitment

3. Successful Marriage-Building Strategies

4. The Complementary Responsibilities of Husbands and Wives

5. Living by Faith

6. Embracing a Sense of Mission

7. Leaving a Spiritual Legacy

Marriage may be under greater attack today than ever before, but God has given us all the resources we need to meet every challenge and thrive, despite them all. In the end, the battle is not ours, but the Lord's—and that is why we can win.

THE LORDSHIP OF CHRIST OVER ALL OF LIFE

THE BIBLE BEGINS with the marriage of a man and a woman and ends with the marriage of Christ and His bride, the Church. In between, God provides timeless blueprints for family life, which, if followed in a spirit of humility and obedience, provide us with the only true way to maintain healthy family relationships.

When Christian couples and their children consistently yield to God's control and power—when they freely, willingly, and joyfully submit to His Lordship over every area of their lives—they will enjoy harmony and deep satisfaction in their marriages and families. Everything else in marriage depends on a clear understanding of why submitting to the lordship of Christ is so vital and why His lordship must extend to every corner of life. For good reason the psalmist reminded us that "the Lord has established his throne in heaven, and his kingdom rules over all" (Ps. 103:19 NIV). Life simply works best when we follow God's plan for our lives, as revealed in the Bible.

1. Read Isaiah 6:1–8

When God called out, "Whom shall I send, and who will go for Us?" Isaiah had a clear choice to make. Would he remain committed to his own concerns, or would he submit himself totally to his Lord? The prophet made his choice when he replied, "Here am I. Send me!" (NASB).

Isaiah understood that God was the Master and he was the servant. He knew that his situation called for total surrender, without reservation. While many see this type of service as lowly—and it *is* humbling—we should consider it a privilege to serve such a loving Lord in every area of our lives . . . including our marriages.

In 1972, the first year of our marriage, Barbara and I decided that before we would give anything to each other, we would surrender our lives, totally and completely, in writing, to Jesus Christ. We gave Him everything we ever dreamed of having. We offered it all up and handed over to Him the title deed to our lives. Today those two title deeds are among the most important papers we have.

That first Christmas together, while Barbara sat down in our kitchen, I went to our sparsely furnished living room and took a seat on the hand-me-down sofa. There we contemplated giving God all that we had and everything we hoped to have as a couple and as a family. She made her list. I made mine.

We gave God what we saw as most important on that day. I gave Him my desires for a successful ministry, nice furniture and things, plenty of money, lasting health, and some good ski equipment. Barbara had a similar list—a house with a fireplace and a bay window, children (at least one boy and one girl) who would honor God, and her rights to be settled and stable.

Looking back, what we signed over to God on that day seems so trivial now, compared to what He has given us. In many instances, He gave us far more than we ever dreamed or imagined. I see that we gave Him only what already belonged to Him: our lives. In return, He has given us "exceeding abundantly above all that we [could] ask or think" (Eph. 3:20 KJV). We humans mistakenly think that surrendering to the God of the universe means the loss of our lives. In reality, total surrender to God brings not total defeat, but total victory!

PONDER ON YOUR OWN

▨ Would you consider giving God, in writing, all that you have and everything you hope to have as a couple and as a family? Explain. What would be on such a list?

DISCUSS WITH YOUR SPOUSE

▨ What does "total surrender" to God mean to each of you?

▨ In what areas of your life together do you most struggle to yield control to God? Explain.

STUDY WITH YOUR GROUP

▨ Discuss this quote: "In reality, total surrender to God brings not total defeat, but total victory!" Does "total surrender" to God scare you? Who that you know seems to exemplify "total surrender" to God? Describe them.

2. Read Luke 10:25–28

For several years as a young man, I allowed God access only to small portions of my life. I went to church and talked about God. But honestly, my heart was far from Him. I'm grateful for a number of events in my life that resulted in spiritual growth. One such incident occurred when I came across a booklet called *My Heart, Christ's Home* that challenged me to give Jesus Christ full control of my life.

The booklet compared the parts of our lives to rooms in a home. Some rooms were open, and Christ had complete access to everything in them. Other rooms, however, declared to God, through shut and bolted doors, "This room is off-limits! This one's *mine!*" As I began to allow Christ access to every room in my heart, liberating changes began to take place in my life.

What about the rooms in your heart? May I challenge you to reflect on His presence in the rooms of your own heart?

Allow Christ to rule the room where you keep your ego. When Jesus isn't allowed in, husbands and wives bicker; children become too competitive and selfish; and everyone is too proud to confess sins.

Open to Christ the room of expectations. With Christ excluded, this room can become filled with longings and unmet hopes—some unrealistic, some that we've never expressed.

Let Christ into the room of relationships with your parents. Too many adults have not fully obeyed the scripture to "leave and cleave" (see Genesis 2:24). Closing off this room to Christ results in unhealthy relationships between adult children and their parents.

What other secret rooms remain off-limits to Him? Lust? An addiction to pornography? A wrong relationship? Open those doors and let Him in.

Christ steps into these rooms with love, forgiveness, and grace. He takes the shame and wipes it clean. He takes the compromises and sets things right. You can trust Him as no house cleaner you've ever had.

PONDER ON YOUR OWN

▓ To what rooms of your heart have you given Christ limited or no access?

DISCUSS WITH YOUR SPOUSE

■ In what areas of your relationship have you given Christ limited or no access? Explain.

STUDY WITH YOUR GROUP

■ Why do so many believers struggle with giving Christ full access to every room of their hearts?

■ How could others make it easier for you to open wide every door of your heart to Christ?

3. Read Deuteronomy 11:13–15

The Christian faith is not a bunch of rules and regulations, but rather a dynamic relationship with the living God, made possible through the work of Jesus Christ. Loving God *fully* is the foundation of a great marriage. When we fully grasp that fact, we are well on our way to living victoriously in every area of our lives.

Loving God wholeheartedly means we obey Him, serve Him, and yield to Him. Totally. That's the only hope that two imperfect people, a husband and a wife, have in truly experiencing all that God has for them. True success in life begins here.

Let's face it—being married isn't always easy. There will be conflicts, illnesses, and external challenges. We need to learn how to fully love God and yield our wills to Him, knowing that He cares for us and that He causes all things to work together for our good and for His glory (see Romans 8:28 and 1 Peter 5:7).

The peace and assurance I need to be a good husband and father don't always come instantly; it's not like flipping on a switch. In the past, I've expected that Christ would *instantly* give me peace and strength to deal with my problems and needs and pressures. But I've learned that coming to Jesus with open hands is just the first step in a long process of learning and receiving from Him.

PONDER ON YOUR OWN

How would you describe your love for God?

DISCUSS WITH YOUR SPOUSE

How can you encourage each other to love God wholeheartedly? What can you start doing? What should you stop doing?

Describe a time in your marriage when you felt God's peace in some difficult situation. What happened?

STUDY WITH YOUR GROUP

In what ways have you seen God work together for your good and His glory? How can such examples encourage you to love God wholeheartedly?

4. Read Leviticus 19:14

I doubt there is any dispute or problem in marriage that can't be solved if both spouses properly fear the Lord and mutually honor and value each other out of that reverential respect for God. A marriage should be a relationship in which forgiveness and acceptance are freely expressed, because we live in His holy presence.

The Bible has a lot to say about the benefits of fearing God. Leviticus 19:14, for example, indicates that a healthy fear of God will motivate us to care for the needs of the disadvantaged. Proverbs 22:4 tells us that fearing God leads us to life, while Proverbs 10:27 tells us that it prolongs life. And Psalm 145:19 says the Lord will fulfill the desires of those who fear Him.

In the New Testament, we see that the fear of God is the glue that holds our relationships—including our marriages—together. Ephesians 5:21 tells us that we should be submitted to one another "*in the fear of God*" (KJV, italics added).

To fear God means that you acknowledge His presence in the midst of everyday choices. Those who fear the Lord apply the Scriptures to effectively meet whatever challenges come their way. Despite their imperfections, they depend on God for strength and find that His power can equip them to meet every challenge.

In a Christian marriage, three are present: the husband, the wife, and Jesus Christ. If the husband and wife share a mutual reverence and a holy desire to obey and serve Christ, then God will use that healthy fear to draw the couple closer to each other and to Himself.

PONDER ON YOUR OWN

■ How do you acknowledge the "fear of the Lord" in your day-to-day life?

DISCUSS WITH YOUR SPOUSE

▓ How does the "fear of the Lord" alter in practical ways your life together?

STUDY WITH YOUR GROUP

▓ What does "the fear of the Lord" mean to you? What doesn't it mean?

▓ Is there a difference between fearing God and being afraid of Him? Explain. Why does the Bible—in both testaments—put such a big emphasis on the fear of the Lord?

5. Read 1 Samuel 2:12–17

The sad story of Eli declares that God is pleased with those who obey Him but opposed to those who defy Him. This is an all-important principle for every couple! We can testify that a couple walking closely with God *knows* and *feels* God's pleasure. God created you to know and to enjoy Him!

When you and your mate experience God, you experience life at its fullest. But when you allow yourselves to drift away from a close walk with Him, life becomes empty and purposeless.

Note how the Bible characterizes the ungodly sons of Eli: "Now the sons of Eli were corrupt; they did not know the Lord" (2:12). These young men—quite religious, but spiritually bankrupt—badly abused their priestly role: "The sin of the young men was very great before the Lord: for men abhorred the offering of the Lord" (v. 17 KJV). The word *abhorred* means "to scorn, feel disgust toward, hate, loathe, abhor, laugh at." Clearly Eli's son's dishonored God with their lives.

God says, "Those who honor Me I will honor, and those who despise Me shall be lightly esteemed" (2:30 NASB). Do you want true joy in your life and marriage? Then honor God. In your lives. In your marriage. In your family. To honor means to "give weight to" or "to value." Honoring God as a couple is the noblest goal you can seek to achieve with your lives.

PONDER ON YOUR OWN

■ What biblical commands regarding marriage do you have the easiest time following? How has this honored God?

■ Practically, how can you as a couple better honor God?

■ What biblical commands regarding marriage do you have the hardest time obeying? What might this say to observers about your relationship with God?

DISCUSS WITH YOUR SPOUSE

■ How joyfully do you find yourself obeying God's commands regarding marriage? How could your obedience as a couple become more joyful?

STUDY WITH YOUR GROUP

■ Why does obedience often take endurance? How can you help each other to endure when obedience gets tough? Give some specifics.

6. Read Judges 17:6; 21:25

The Old Testament describes many difficult periods and dark days in the history of Israel. Of one particularly bad time, it was written, "In those days there was no king in Israel; everyone did what was right in his own eyes."

That sounds very much like our culture today, doesn't it? We live in a time when moral, spiritual, or social absolutes seem in very short supply. Each person can freely define his or her own set of values and morals.

Our culture despises the idea of pushing one's own values on someone else. Even many Christians have adopted this attitude—which is tragic, because followers of Christ are to broadcast the values of Scripture and the gospel of Christ. While room certainly exists for individuals to apply differing interpretations to some parts of the Bible, many scriptural values should be clear to all.

We need to ask ourselves, "Whose values are most important to us?" and "What are the values we ultimately embrace in our family?" If we answer with anything but those spelled out in the written Word of God, then it is past time for some personal reevaluation and change.

PONDER ON YOUR OWN

■ Where do you see moral relativism, people lowering their standards to fit in with the culture? How has it affected you?

DISCUSS WITH YOUR SPOUSE

Whose values are most important to you? What values do you ultimately embrace in your family? How are these values worked out in lifestyle choices?

STUDY WITH YOUR GROUP

What examples have you seen of our culture despising the idea of pushing one's own values on others? How have you responded to these incidents?

What scriptural values do you think should be "clear to all"?

7. Read Numbers 22:1–35

It is important that we learn to discern God's will for our lives. As the apostle Paul wrote, "Do not be unwise, but understand what the will of the Lord is" (Eph. 5:17).

Repeatedly in the Old Testament we see men and women whom God placed in positions of responsibility. When they arrived at a fork in the road and had to make a key decision, however, many failed to ask God what they should do. Scripture teaches that a person who fails to consult God on decisions and directions is a fool.

Balaam may be one of the prime examples of this. Although the Lord truly did speak through him, he got sidetracked by a lust for money (see 2 Peter 2:15). He wandered so far off track, in fact, that God resorted to speaking to him through his own donkey to restrain "the madness of the prophet" (v. 16 NASB).

God may test us with what looks like a small decision, but in reality it may be one of the most important choices of our lives. Do you want God's will in just the big decisions, or in the little ones as well? The Christian life is composed of both! Cultivate the daily habit of seeking God's will through His Word and prayer in every decision you face.

PONDER ON YOUR OWN

▣ How important to you is discovering God's will for your life? How do you try to find His will?

DISCUSS WITH YOUR SPOUSE

▣ What do think is God's will for your marriage right now? What major decisions do you face? How do you plan to go about making those decisions?

STUDY WITH YOUR GROUP

▣ Describe a time when you believe God may have been testing you with some decision. What happened? What did you learn?

▣ How have you used God's Word and prayer to find God's will for some specific challenge facing you? Describe the process.

8. Read Job 38:1–13

When God finally answered Job out of the whirlwind, He answered the anguished man's questions with some much harder questions of His own. In the spirit of hard questions, I have a few I'd like to ask of the contemporary church:

- Why is the divorce rate inside the church nearly identical to the divorce rate outside the church?

- Why do so many Christian men perform aggressively at work and remain so disengaged and passive at home?

- Why are so many Christian parents negative about having and rearing children?

- Why do so many Christians say their secular job is their ministry, but then show so little fruit for their efforts?

- Why do Christians talk about family values while their lifestyles look virtually identical to the average non-Christian's?

- Why have so many Christians in full-time ministry washed out because of immorality and impurity?

- Why is the fifth commandment—to honor our parents—neglected by large numbers of Christians?

- Why do fewer than 10 percent of all Christians regularly tell others about God's forgiveness and the new life found in Christ?

- If Jesus Christ changes lives, then why do 50 million Americans claiming to be born again have such a marginal impact on society?

I believe the answer to each of these questions can be tied to a failure to obey and take seriously the lordship of Christ in our lives. When we learn to humbly trust and obey God, He brings personal transformation. And that's how cultures get changed—one person and one home at a time.

PONDER ON YOUR OWN

Which of the questions above make you the most uncomfortable? Why?

DISCUSS WITH YOUR SPOUSE

How is your home helping to change the ungodly culture around you?

STUDY WITH YOUR GROUP

How does our culture make it difficult to "take seriously the lordship of Christ"? How can you help each other overcome that difficulty?

Respond to this question: "Why do fewer than 10 percent of all Christians regularly tell others about God's forgiveness and the new life found in Christ?" When did you last tell someone? What happened?

9. Read Mark 1:16–18

Jesus lived, taught, and led with authority. We see a good picture of this as we read what happened when He called Simon and Andrew to follow Him. They didn't take a few days to figure out what it would cost them to follow, or to ask their father if it was okay for them to go. No, "they immediately left their nets and followed Him." They *heard* the voice of Jesus and *acted*.

Peter and Andrew dropped everything and followed Jesus that day for one reason: He had authority to call them—the same authority He has today.

One reason why we don't see more people leaving their nets and following Christ is that we in the church have not presented Jesus in all of His splendor and authority. When people start to see Jesus in all His majesty, they will respond much as Simon and Andrew did.

Jesus calls each of us as individuals, as couples, and as families to become "fishers of men" (v. 17), and only when we obey His calling will we see our households effectively influence our neighborhoods and our towns for Christ.

PONDER ON YOUR OWN

How did you hear the call of Jesus to follow Him? How has following Him changed your life?

How effective do you think you are at influencing your neighborhood and town for Christ? Explain.

DISCUSS WITH YOUR SPOUSE

What kind of authority does Jesus Christ have in your home? How does this authority show itself in your daily living? How much of Christ's authority and majesty would a guest in your home see by observing your everyday activity?

STUDY WITH YOUR GROUP

■ How can you help and encourage each other to become more effective at influencing your neighborhoods and town for Christ?

10. Read John 6:47–68

When we see Jesus for who He really is, no possession, no worldly honor or success, can compare with the King of kings.

So why doesn't everyone follow Him? John 6 records that after Christ made some difficult and challenging statements, "many of His disciples went back and walked with Him no more" (v. 66). So Jesus said to the remaining twelve, "Do you also want to go away?" (v. 67). Peter gave a profound reply: "Lord, to whom shall we go? You have the words of eternal life" (v. 68). Peter saw no one else worthy of following.

Peter's opinion did not change in the subsequent weeks, months, and years. After Jesus rose from the grave and the Holy Spirit came to dwell in the church at Pentecost, Peter stood up in front of the Jewish religious leaders and declared, "Nor is there salvation in any other, for there is no other name under heaven given among men by which we must be saved" (Acts 4:12).

The longer I live, the more I see that *nothing matters more than Jesus Christ and His Word.* In recent days I've asked Him to reinfuse my life with the conviction that He alone is worth following. I have been following Christ since 1968, and I have absolutely no regrets. Because He is alive, He can and does bring purpose to my life. He instructs me. He corrects me. He forgives me. He guides me. He comforts me. He disciplines me. He loves me. He prays for me. And He is coming back for me.

It doesn't get any better than that.

PONDER ON YOUR OWN

▨ How do you respond to Jesus when He says "hard things" to you? What are some of the hardest things He has said to you?

▨ In what ways does your life differ from someone who does not follow Jesus?

DISCUSS WITH YOUR SPOUSE

▨ How does Jesus bring purpose to your life as a married couple? In what ways has Jesus been instructing you lately? In what areas has He corrected you? Where is He guiding you right now as a family? Through what means has He comforted you? How has His discipline changed the way you live? How does He show His love for you?

STUDY WITH YOUR GROUP

▨ Discuss the following quote: "Nothing matters more than Jesus Christ and His Word." Do you agree? Why or why not? If you agree, how does your agreement change the way you live? How can outsiders identify you as a follower of Jesus?

MARRIAGE AS A COVENANT COMMITMENT

THE TRADITIONAL WEDDING VOWS used by most couples constitute a covenantal oath, not a two-party contract. The vows I shared with Barbara went like this: "I, Dennis, take you, Barbara, to be my lawfully wedded wife. I promise and covenant, before God and these witnesses, to be your loving and faithful husband; to stand by you in riches and in poverty, in joy and in sorrow, in sickness and in health, forsaking all others, as long as we both shall live."

When we spoke these words, Barbara and I weren't agreeing to provide some personal services via a contract that could be terminated if either of us defaulted. Instead, we were entering into a covenant—the same type of sacred, binding obligation that God made with His children on several momentous occasions, for instance, with Noah after the flood.

Marriage is not a private experiment, littered with prenuptial agreements and an attitude of "Try it! If it doesn't work, you can always bail out." Marriage is not a convenient relationship based on "What's in it for me?" And marriage is not some kind of social contract, something you do only "for as long as you both shall live and *love*."

Marriage is a sacred, lifetime covenant between one man and one woman and their God. It is a public vow of how you will relate to your spouse as you form a new family unit. It is solemn, significant, and holy.

While our culture no longer takes marriage seriously, God takes the wedding covenant—and the vows we make to one another—*very* seriously. Fulfill your vows!

1. Read Proverbs 20:25

When couples speak their vows to each other during the wedding ceremony, they pledge to faithfully enter the estate of *holy* matrimony. It's holy because God has set it apart and blessed it. The Old Testament declares, "For the Lord God of Israel says that He hates divorce" (Mal. 2:16), and in the New Testament, Jesus proclaimed, "Therefore what God has joined together, let not man separate" (Matt. 19:6). As others have so rightly pointed out, the Lord didn't stutter when He spoke these words!

Any covenant—including the marriage covenant—is a binding, weighty obligation. It is time for us to embrace and proclaim God's sacred view of marriage, as well as His holy hatred for divorce.

We can do that best by first committing our marriages to the Lord. God wants to demonstrate to the world through our marriages that He is indeed alive and active in this most important of all human relationships.

Second, we do this by helping others succeed at marriage. We live in a culture that not only accepts divorce, but expects it. Why not try to come alongside friends or family members who are having difficulty in their marriages? Too many marriages dissolve over what ultimately are insignificant matters. We all need cheerleaders and coaches. Why not become one?

PONDER ON YOUR OWN

■ What does the idea of "holy" matrimony mean to you? How does it make a difference in the way you relate to your own marriage?

DISCUSS WITH YOUR SPOUSE

■ How have you committed your marriage to the Lord? What can you do to remind each other of that commitment?

■ What kind of help might you need in your marriage? What kind of help could you give other married couples?

STUDY WITH YOUR GROUP

■ How can you come alongside friends who are struggling in their marriages? How can you do this without being overbearing or intrusive?

2. Read Matthew 19:4–6

Everyone must adjust to qualities in a spouse that went unnoticed or got ignored during the dreamy days of dating. How many individuals have encountered a painful frustration in marriage and asked themselves, *Why did I do this? Did I marry the wrong person?*

When these questions arise, you need to confront them immediately. If you don't resolve these doubts promptly, they will hang around indefinitely, like a dark and distant cloud on the horizon of your relationship.

If you find yourself struggling with these questions, go back to the admonition in Genesis 2:24, 25, where spouses are commanded to leave, cleave, become one flesh, and be completely transparent with each other. If such doubts bother you, face them by getting away alone for a weekend to seek out the Lord and pray for His peace on this matter.

Let me assure you that you *are* married to the right person. How do I know this? Because God hates divorce, and He wants your marriage to last!

You may have gone against some biblical admonitions in getting to where you are, but the Scripture is clear: Do *not* try to undo a "mistake" and, in the process, make a second one. (See 1 Corinthians 7:10, 27.)

PONDER ON YOUR OWN

■ What can you do to prove that *you* are the "right one" for your spouse?

■ What frustrations in your marriage prompt you to wonder about whether you made the right choice of a mate? What can you do to immediately combat these feelings of frustration?

DISCUSS WITH YOUR SPOUSE

■ Name several reasons you know your spouse is exactly the right one for you.

STUDY WITH YOUR GROUP

■ How would you answer someone who said, "I'm not happy in this marriage, and I know God wants me happy. Therefore, divorce is what's best for me"?

3. Read Genesis 2:24

You may have moved out of their house a long time ago, but have you *really* left your parents behind?

God did not mince words when He instructed married couples to leave their parents. The Hebrew word normally translated *leave* from Genesis 2:24 more fully means "to forsake dependence upon," "lose," "leave behind," "release," and "let go."

Centuries later, Jesus addressed this issue when He said that God never intended for *anybody*—not in-laws, mother, father, children, friends, pastors, or employers—to come between a husband and a wife (Matt. 19:6). *No one!*

After our wedding ceremony, Barbara and I walked down the aisle together, symbolically proclaiming to all witnesses that we had left our parents. We had forsaken our dependence upon them for our livelihood and emotional support, and were turning now to each other—for the rest of our lives—as the most important persons in our universe. This public affirmation of our covenant to each other meant, "No relationship on earth, other than my relationship with Jesus Christ and God, is more important to me than the one with my spouse."

If you or your spouse has not fully left mother and father, begin to discuss how you have failed to leave and what you can do today to truly forsake dependence upon your parents and cleave to one another.

PONDER ON YOUR OWN

Why is it so necessary for couples to leave their parents? What can happen to the new marriage when this "leaving" remains incomplete?

DISCUSS WITH YOUR SPOUSE

Has each of you truly left your mother and father? Gently explore any areas of life—financial, emotional, social—where there still may be some "leaving" to do.

STUDY WITH YOUR GROUP

■ How can unbiblical attitudes toward a couple's children sometimes get in the way of that couple's "cleaving"? What suggestions might you have to avoid this problem?

■ How can you make your spouse "the most important person in the universe" to you? What can you start doing? What can you stop doing?

4. Read Isaiah 38:3

All husbands and wives have expectations of how the wedded relationship should work. They often assume, "My spouse will meet me halfway." Over the years we've heard couples talk about having a 50/50 marriage. *You do your part*, the thinking goes, *and I'll do mine*. But while this concept sounds logical, couples who try to live it out are destined for disappointment.

Why does the 50/50 marriage idea inevitably fail? For one reason, we tend to focus more on what the *other* person is giving than on what *we* are doing. So we withhold love until the other person meets our expectations. It's impossible, of course, to know if a person has ever met you halfway. As seventeenth-century author Thomas Fuller said, "Every horse thinks his own pack heaviest."

Early in our marriage, we tried this plan. I would give affection to Barbara only when I felt she had earned it. Barbara would show me love and offer praise only when she thought I had held up my end of things.

Contrast this with the type of love God shows for us. No matter what we do, He gives us 100 percent. He shows us love even though we don't deserve it!

So I propose that couples adopt the 100/100 plan in marriage. Under this plan, each person gives 100 percent . . . no matter what the other person does.

PONDER ON YOUR OWN

▉ What expectations did you have of your marriage on your wedding day? How have these expectations changed?

DISCUSS WITH YOUR SPOUSE

▉ Have you ever related to each other with the expectation, "My spouse is supposed to meet me halfway"? Explain.

▉ How practical is the 100/100 plan in marriage? Explain. What would it take for it to work?

STUDY WITH YOUR GROUP

▉ In what ways have you seen a spouse (not necessarily your own) withhold love because of some unmet expectation? What generally happens in such a scenario?

5. Read Ezekiel 16:6–8

Several years ago, God gave us the wonderful privilege of helping a couple resurrect a marriage that seemed beyond hope. Their real commitment to Christ and to each other caused them to grow steadily in their relationship, bringing dramatic changes to their home.

But one day the wife came to us, discouraged once more about her marriage. Apparently she and her husband had reached an impasse. Each time they argued about the problem, the husband threatened to leave, a tactic from the past. He saturated their relationship with the fear that maybe he would follow through this time.

We often tell people that one of the "ten commandments of marriage" should be *Never threaten to leave*. As for so many areas of the Christian life, God gave us a memorable example to follow. Over and over in Scripture He tells us that He loves us, that He's committed to us, that He will never leave us nor forsake us. (See, for example, John 3:16; Hebrews 13:5.)

Speak such loving, reassuring words to your mate. Regularly repeat your commitment, describe your love, and offer potent word pictures of your determination to stick together, regardless of what comes.

And when some problem does arise—and it will!—use the incident as yet another opportunity to reassure your spouse (even in the heat of battle) that your commitment to the marriage and to the relationship remains firm, solid, and secure.

PONDER ON YOUR OWN

■ Have you ever threatened to leave your mate? Explain. Do you ever emotionally leave your mate by withdrawing for an extended period of time because of conflict? Explain.

■ How secure do you believe your mate feels in your commitment to your marriage? Explain. Are you more committed to your mate than to your career? your children? your hobbies and favorite activities? How do you think your mate would answer each of these questions?

DISCUSS WITH YOUR SPOUSE

Why not write a letter that tells your spouse you would marry him or her all over again? Then read your note to your spouse and thank God for giving you your mate, no matter what problems you may face. Finish by reaffirming your marriage covenant with God together in prayer.

STUDY WITH YOUR GROUP

What are some ways that the marriage is affected when one spouse keeps divorce as an option? What might happen in the marriage if the option of divorce is taken away? When a couple is having a serious conflict, how are they helped by knowing that there is no threat of divorce?

6. Read Exodus 20:14

For too many people, Christians included, adultery is the first step out of a marriage. An emotional or sexual attachment to someone other than your spouse creates intense passions that sabotage trust and steal marital intimacy.

Adultery destroys homes and lives. As alluring as it may seem, adultery always fails to live up to its promises. It pledges excitement and fulfillment, and instead delivers pain and alienation. The grass is *not* greener on the other side of the fence! The glistening highway of adultery is actually a rutted back road littered with loneliness, guilt, and broken hearts. Adultery supplants loyalty and trust with fear and suspicion. The consequences are enormous and last for a lifetime.

Will you commit to emotional and moral fidelity to your spouse, no matter how much you struggle in your marriage? If so, three steps are critical:

First, *maintain a healthy sexual relationship.* Lovingly study your mate to learn what will keep him or her interested and satisfied in the bedroom.

Cultivate the fine—and often forgotten—art of romance. Pursue your spouse with the same creativity and energy that characterized your dating relationship.

Second, *guard your heart in relation to the opposite sex.* According to Jesus, the eyes are the doorway to the heart (Matt. 6:22, 23). For this reason, restrict your gaze and refuse the temptation to look longingly at other men or women. Don't fantasize about someone else.

Third, *be honest with your spouse about temptations.* One of the most important practices Barbara and I employed early in our marriage was that of sharing with each other when we felt tempted.

PONDER ON YOUR OWN

■ Have you committed to emotional and moral fidelity to your spouse? When? In what ways?

DISCUSS WITH YOUR SPOUSE

■ How healthy is your sexual relationship? What can you do together to make it healthier?

■ What temptations cause each of you the most struggle? What can you do to help each other overcome these temptations?

STUDY WITH YOUR GROUP

■ Discuss some effective strategies for "guarding your heart" against the possibility of adultery. What have you seen work?

7. Read 2 Kings 19

Your covenant of commitment to God and each other is what remains after reality has edited what you *thought* marriage would be. Think back to your wedding. You stood before God at the altar and promised never to leave or forsake your spouse, in sickness and in health, for better or for worse. When you stare "worse" in the face, you have a choice.

Will you honor that commitment?

At this crossroads, you can reject your vows, believing there is no hope; or you can trust God, believing that He is able to help you rekindle the smoldering ashes and transform them into something vibrant.

When King Hezekiah faced disaster at the hands of the invading Assyrians, he humbly turned to God for rescue—and God erased the Assyrian threat. The same thing can happen in your marriage! As some dear friends said to us when we reached a very difficult time of testing in our family, "What an awesome opportunity to see God work!"

Your marriage will face some challenging seasons. All marriages do. When you trust God to renew your commitment to one another and to rekindle your romance, you set your marriage on a course to experience the season of mature, committed love. This season is well worth the work! We know. We've experienced it.

PONDER ON YOUR OWN

■ What "worse" have you already had to deal with in your marriage? How have you dealt with it? How can you trust God and tap into His power to deal with it more effectively?

DISCUSS WITH YOUR SPOUSE

■ In what area(s) of your marriage do you see an awesome opportunity for God to work?

■ Try to picture for one another what the "season of mature, committed love" might look like for you. How can you work today for this season tomorrow?

STUDY WITH YOUR GROUP

■ Recount several stories in which a couple you know of was able to "rekindle the smoldering ashes" of their marriage "and transform them into something vibrant."

8. Read John 16:32, 33

Modern society still suffers from the sickness of the "Me Generation," which since the '60s has contaminated the covenant of marriage. The selfish, Me-Gen person says, in effect, "When marriage serves my purposes, I'm on board. When it ceases to make me happy, when it's too much effort, when the unexpected shows up and creates pressure, then I'm out of here." Some leave physically and move out, while others leave emotionally and withdraw.

Your vows mean your commitment will endure. When the pressure becomes relentless, white-hot, and intense, when the cultural voices around you entice you to look out for yourself and quit your marriage, your vows should scream, "DON'T!" The fact that we will not quit, that we will be there for one another, even when the unexpected happens, helps to mitigate the pressure between us.

Besides, why are we so surprised when trouble comes our way? Jesus actually *promised* we would experience problems. "In the world," He said, "you *will* have tribulation" (italics added). Then in the next breath, He quickly pointed out, "But be of good cheer, I have overcome the world."

Expect the unexpected: suffering, trials, difficulty. But don't give up! Jesus will be there in the midst of your troubles. And you can be there for one another too. The marriage covenant creates security and safety for a husband and a wife amid life's storms. That's one of the blessings of the covenant commitment of marriage.

PONDER ON YOUR OWN

How have cultural pressures—especially those that scream for you to look out for yourself—caused difficulties in your marriage? How have you responded to these pressures?

DISCUSS WITH YOUR SPOUSE

How can the two of you help one another prepare for the unexpected? What have you learned from watching how others have dealt with their challenges?

STUDY WITH YOUR GROUP

■ What does it mean to you that Jesus has promised not only that you will suffer hardships, but that He will be there with you in those hardships? How can this promise become something more than a comforting religious platitude?

■ Look up some other Bible passages that warn of various kinds of hardship for believers. What do these verses tell you about life and about marriage?

9. Read Micah 7:18, 19

If you accept your mate only in part, you can love him or her only in part. That's why unconditionally accepting your mate is so important.

While serving aboard a gunboat in Vietnam, Dave Roever was holding a phosphorus grenade some six inches from his face when a sniper's bullet ignited the explosive. The first time he saw himself after the explosion, he says he saw a monster, not a human being. "I was alone in the way the souls in hell must feel alone," he wrote.[1]

When he returned to the States, he feared how his young bride, Brenda, would react. He had just watched a wife tell another burn victim that she wanted a divorce. But when Brenda walked in, she kissed him on what was left of his face, smiled, and said, "Welcome home, Davey! I love you."

That's what marriage is all about. Marriage is another person being committed enough to you to accept the real you, scars and all. It means two people working together to heal their deepest wounds. It means following God's example in our marriage: "He will again have compassion on us, and will subdue our iniquities. You will cast all our sins into the depths of the sea."

PONDER ON YOUR OWN

▨ What does unconditionally accepting your mate mean to you? How are you working toward unconditionally accepting your mate?

DISCUSS WITH YOUR SPOUSE

▨ How did each of you react to the Dave Roever story? Discuss your responses.

▨ Which of your own "scars" do you fear your mate might have trouble accepting? Explain. Then pray with one another for a spirit of unconditional acceptance.

STUDY WITH YOUR GROUP

▨ How have you and your spouse worked together to heal your deepest wounds? How can others help you in this process? How can you use your experience to help others?

10. Read Leviticus 26:3–9

Understanding and agreeing to the covenant aspect of marriage is one thing; living it out is quite another. Consider five ideas that will make a covenantal commitment a reality in your marriage.

1. *Pray together every day as a couple.* When Barbara and I first were married, I asked a man I highly respected for his best counsel on marriage. "I've prayed every day with my, Sara Jo, for more than twenty-five years," he told me. "Nothing has built our marriage more than our prayer time together."

   Barbara and I usually pray together before going to sleep, but on some nights neither of us has felt like praying. The Lord has gently reminded me, *You need to pray with her.* And even though on occasion I haven't even wanted to *talk* to her, I have finally rolled over and said, "Let's pray." Our practice of this spiritual discipline has reminded us of the real Source of strength in our marriage and has kept us connected and communicating.

2. *Never use the* D *word.* Marriage is tough, and at times every one of us probably has thought about giving up. The key word is *thought.* No matter how hopeless the situation seems or how lousy you feel, I urge you not to *say* the D word—divorce—in your home. Words have power. If you first think about divorce and then talk about it, before long, what once was unthinkable becomes an option.

3. *Sign a marriage covenant.* Whether you are newlyweds or have been married for years, why not consider having a covenant-signing ceremony? You could do this with other couples at your church or in your home, with witnesses from your family or close friends.

4. *Do what you promised.* It won't make any difference if you sign a piece of paper but later break your covenant. Don't let temptations and conflicts keep you from finishing strong in your marriage and family. Don't let go! Fulfill your vows.

5. *Urge others to keep their covenants.* We need to band together in the Christian community to stand for marital commitment and to fight divorce. We need to combat divorce in the most positive way—by honoring our covenants and encouraging others to do the same.

PONDER ON YOUR OWN

■ What do you think about each of the five recommendations outlined above? Will you commit to going through with them? Why or why not?

DISCUSS WITH YOUR SPOUSE

■ If you regularly pray with one another, what do each of you find the most encouraging about the practice? If you do not regularly pray with one another, what keeps you from doing so?

STUDY WITH YOUR GROUP

■ Discuss the possibilities of having your group schedule a "covenant-signing ceremony." When and how could you do it? Who would you invite?

■ What can you do as a group to encourage others to keep their marital commitment? Who do you know that could use such encouragement right now?

SUCCESSFUL MARRIAGE-BUILDING STRATEGIES

ALL INTIMATE RELATIONSHIPS begin with transparency. Here's how the Bible describes transparency in marriage before the Fall: "And they were both naked, the man and his wife, and were not ashamed" (Gen. 2:25).

Before Adam and Eve sinned against God, they wore no disguise or covering, used no mask. They were uncovered physically and had no need to cover up emotionally. They couldn't and wouldn't hide anything from one another. Adam and Eve served as a picture of true transparency. They were *real* with one another, open to one another, and unafraid of rejection.

But this transparency totally changed after the Fall: "Then the eyes of both of them were opened, and they knew that they were naked; and they sewed fig leaves together and made themselves coverings" (3:7). Sin introduced a lot more than a need for modesty. It also brought deceit, lying, half-truths, manipulation, misrepresentation, hatred, jealousy, and control, all prompting us to wear masks.

God's plan for marriage continues to be transparency and openness. And by obeying His Word through the power of the Spirit, we can experience the joys of His plan once more.

KEEP COMMUNICATION ALIVE

1. Read Romans 15:23, 24

Isolation and the failure to communicate drain the life from relationships. Most people long for intimacy and fellowship, but without communication, these two relationship essentials remain out of reach.

The apostle Paul was a single man, but he understood the vital role of communication in any relationship. So he made a point to tell the Roman Christians of his "great desire these many years" to visit them and promised, "Whenever I journey to Spain, I shall come to you." He didn't want them to guess about his affection for them; he wanted them to hear it straight from his own heart.

Your marriage depends on your willingness to communicate. It is the only way you can cultivate the intimacy and fellowship that God intends a husband and wife to share within a marriage.

A marriage with Christ at its center can be a safe place to learn how to communicate. And a family with a great model of communication provides the very best training ground for children to learn what true communication looks like.

PONDER ON YOUR OWN

- Recall an example from your family of origin when a lack of communication created a problem. What happened? Was it resolved? If so, how? If not, why not?

DISCUSS WITH YOUR SPOUSE

▨ How can you and your spouse work together to take practical steps to improve your communication? Does one of you need to talk less and listen more? Does the other need to work at disclosing what is going on in his or her life?

▨ Take an extended time to pray that the lines of communication be opened and remain open between you two, so that your relationships with God, each other, and your children will flourish.

STUDY WITH YOUR GROUP

▨ Spend an evening discussing how you can better communicate with your spouse. Share ideas and talk about what you've seen that "works."

2. Read Genesis 42:21–23

When Joseph's brothers came from Canaan to Egypt, seeking food in the midst of a great famine, they used an interpreter to communicate with their brother. At times in our marriage, Barbara and I have needed someone to interpret for us so we could truly understand each other! Understanding is not merely a transfer of information, but empathy for the other person, based on what he or she communicated.

Barbara and I have found understanding to be essential in building each other's self-image. We are continually seeking to comprehend the context of each other's lives, which helps to explain our self-image, our behavior, and our attitudes.

Applying this "law of understanding" will give you the right to be heard by your mate. If he or she senses that you truly understand—or at least *desire* to understand—then your suggestions and attempts to build into your mate will be better received.

Proverbs 24:3 reads, "Through wisdom a house is built, and by understanding it is established." And 1 Peter 3:7 teaches husbands to dwell with their wives with understanding. As we give each other the gift of understanding, we build a stronger, healthier marriage that endures.

PONDER ON YOUR OWN

■ The next time your mate expresses a concern, ask if he or she feels that you understand it. Practice listening with a sympathetic ear, and look beyond the response to its cause. What has occurred in your mate's life that contributes to this present attitude? Which pressures today may be crushing your mate's self-confidence?

DISCUSS WITH YOUR SPOUSE

■ How well do you feel you two are getting along? What do you think you could do together to improve your relationship through better communication?

■ Ask each other the following questions: "Have I ever made a promise to you that I didn't keep? Do you feel that I respect you? Is there some secret you are keeping from me, out of fear that I would love you less? What can I do to show you that I want to be more like Christ? Is there something I do that annoys or embarrasses you? How could I best express to you just how much I love you, and how honored I feel to be your mate?"

STUDY WITH YOUR GROUP

■ Discuss Proverbs 24:3 and 1 Peter 3:7. What do these texts teach you about communication? How can you better put them into practice? What difficulties do you anticipate in applying them? How can you successfully overcome these difficulties?

BE DILIGENT TO RESOLVE CONFLICT

1. Read Ephesians 4:32; Matthew 18:22; 1 Peter 1:6, 7

There's nothing worse than lying in the darkness, back to back, and fuming about some petty argument. Satan is out to destroy marriages, and one of his best tools is *unresolved conflict*. No wonder Paul urged believers, "Be kind to one another, tenderhearted, forgiving one another, even as God in Christ forgave you" (Eph. 4:32).

How did Christ forgive us? By laying down His life. He didn't wait until we apologized. He took the initiative to forgive. I should do the same, even when I (Barbara) feel my husband is clearly in the wrong. Sometimes it's much easier for me to see only what *he* did wrong than it is for me to admit my part in the conflict.

When conflict arises, I must resist my tendency to run *from* a confrontation and, instead, run *toward* forgiveness. I must choose to listen, to imagine how my husband feels, and to pray for wisdom, understanding, and God's help to work it all out. For the sake of your marriage, forgive "not . . . up to seven times, but up to seventy times seven" (Matt. 18:22). Forgiveness guards our hearts from bitterness and creates fertile soil in which romance and love can grow.

And remember this: as difficult as it can be to work through conflict, we can claim God's promises as we do so. God wants to use our conflicts to test our faith, to produce endurance, to refine us, and to bring glory to Himself (1 Peter 1:6, 7). This process isn't easy! It can be like a fire hot enough to melt gold—yet note the results. When you pass the test, your faith is "much more precious than gold"!

PONDER ON YOUR OWN

How do you tend to react to conflict? Do you run away from it or run toward forgiveness? Explain.

DISCUSS WITH YOUR SPOUSE

How do the two of you usually deal with conflict? How could you improve the way you manage your conflicts?

Think back to a conflict that has since been resolved, how could you have shown more kindness to one another? How could you have been more tenderhearted? Would remembering that "God in Christ forgave you" have helped you forgive each other? Knowing that you will have other conflicts in the future, discuss some strategies for putting these scriptural principles into practical action.

STUDY WITH YOUR GROUP

How has God used marital conflict to test your faith? What have you learned from these times of testing?

2. Read Judges 6:11–16

Barbara and I manage our conflicts with a tool we call "loving confrontation." When either of us gets upset with the other, we try not to hide or deny what is making us see red; we get the hurt in the open through direct, but loving confrontation.

If you want to practice loving confrontation, you can't believe your mate is out to get you, nor can you be out to get your mate. Be willing to hear what God may be saying through your mate. Many of Barbara's best statements to me hurt a bit; but I need to hear them because they keep me on the right track. I want to hear what she is trying to say, instead of plotting how I will defend myself. Consider a few tips that Barbara and I have found useful in keeping a judgmental spirit out of confrontation:

Check your motivation. Will what you say help or hurt? Will bringing this up cause healing, wholeness, and oneness, or further conflict?

Check your attitude. A tender spirit expressed through loving confrontation says, "I care about you. I respect you, and I want you to respect me. I want to know how you feel." Don't hop on your bulldozer and run down your partner.

Check the circumstances. The circumstances may include timing, location, and setting. Barbara should not confront me as I walk in the house after a hard day's work; I should not confront her as she's helping a sick child.

Check to determine what other pressures may be present. Be sensitive to where your mate is coming from. What's the context of your mate's life right now?

Check your readiness to take it as well as dish it out. Sometimes a confrontation can boomerang. Your mate may have some "stuff" saved on the other side of the fence that will suddenly come right back at you.

Check the emotional temperature. Call a time-out if the conflict escalates. Hot, emotionally charged words don't bring peace. Say, "I'm not running away from our talk. I love you and want to work this out—but I need a little time to process before we continue our conversation."

PONDER ON YOUR OWN

▇ Prayer is often the best barometer of your motivation. Think of your last conflict with your spouse. Take that situation to God and ask Him to shine His light on you and the problem. What do you learn of your motivation?

▇ In most of your conflicts with your spouse, do you have a spirit of humility or pride? Explain.

DISCUSS WITH YOUR SPOUSE

▇ How can you better practice direct, open, loving confrontation with one another? What skills do you need to acquire? What skills do you need to improve? What tactics do you need to abandon?

STUDY WITH YOUR GROUP

▇ How do the couples in your group approach conflict resolution? Discuss the strengths and weaknesses of each approach mentioned. Also, discuss the methods suggested on page 49 and consider especially how each approach might work in your own case.

PRAY TOGETHER AS A COUPLE

1. Read Psalm 32:6

Scripture gives several compelling reasons for couples to faithfully and regularly pray together. Barbara and I have found that the more we put these into practice, the closer we come to one another and to the Lord.

First, we are commanded to pray. Jesus said we are to pray at all times and "not lose heart" (Luke 18:1). Paul told us to "pray without ceasing" (1 Thess. 5:17). If you are a believer in Christ, then prayer should define your life.

Second, through prayer we meet with God and build a relationship with Him. What an unspeakable honor to come boldly into the presence of the Creator of the universe! The Scriptures tell us that God inhabits the praises of His people (see Psalm 22:3 KJV). God delights in hearing us acknowledge His goodness, character, and kindness. One wife told us, "Prayer together helps keep God in the center." Through prayer, God comes to dwell in the middle of your marriage and family!

Third, in prayer we have the opportunity to confess (and repent of) our sins to God and receive a clean conscience (1 John 1:9).

Fourth, through prayer we receive answers and wisdom from the Lord (James 1:5). God delights in giving you the insights you need to handle the problems you face.

Finally, prayer lightens our load. Jesus said, "Come to Me, all who labor and are heavy laden, and I will give you rest" (Matt. 11:28). Prayer is a very practical way to exchange your worries for peace (Phil. 4:6, 7).

PONDER ON YOUR OWN

What do you find most challenging about praying with your spouse? What benefits have you experienced through such joint prayer sessions? What, if anything, keeps you from praying together more often?

DISCUSS WITH YOUR SPOUSE

▨ What issues currently facing you could best be addressed through joint prayer?

▨ When is the best time for you to pray together? When is the worst time? What practical steps can you take, starting today, to enhance your prayer times together?

STUDY WITH YOUR GROUP

▨ From your experience and reading of Scripture, what do you know of prayer? What Bible passages on prayer resonate most strongly with you? Why? What can you teach each others about some effective ways of praying with your spouse? What advice would you give about traps or difficulties to avoid?

2. Read Psalm 107:1

Some time ago a couple told us, "It is as important to pray thankfully during times of pain or when begging God for help as it is during times of joy. God blesses a joyful heart!"

In 1 Thessalonians 5:18 we learn to give thanks in *everything*, "for this is the will of God in Christ Jesus for you." We have learned to give thanks for:

- good days and bad

- good health and chronic disease

- problems at work, with a child, with a parent, or with a neighbor

- flat tires, umpires with seemingly poor vision at Little League games, teenage attitudes, and vacation days gone awry.

When we give thanks in all things, we see more clearly how God is involved in every part of our lives. We are also reminded that He is in control. As Barbara and I have practiced giving thanks continually over the years, it has become easier and easier.

Why does God want us to be thankful through all circumstances and conditions?

First, giving thanks expresses faith—faith in our God, who is competent and never makes a mistake. He can be trusted!

Second, we quickly begin to exhibit more of the fruits of righteousness (see Galatians 5:22, 23). As we yield to His Spirit, we become more and more of what the Bible calls a spiritual person (see 1 Corinthians 2:14, 15).

Third, God wants us to move beyond the small stuff, because He has big stuff for us to do on His behalf. If we spend our lives overwhelmed with the details of daily existence, how will we ever become warriors for the big causes of Jesus Christ?

Learning the art of giving thanks as a twosome is one of the most rewarding experiences of praying together.

PONDER ON YOUR OWN

■ When did you last give thanks with your spouse for something God did for you? Describe it.

■ Do you see yourself as a "spiritual person," biblically speaking? Why or why not?

DISCUSS WITH YOUR SPOUSE

■ Individually write down a list of things for which you are thankful, exchange the completed lists, and finally, give thanks together in prayer for those things.

STUDY WITH YOUR GROUP

■ What "big stuff" do you think God might be asking you to do, or to prepare for, on His behalf? How can your group encourage you in this?

LEARN TO GROW STRONGER THROUGH SUFFERING

1. Read Jeremiah 38:6

Hardships, troubles, and difficulties elbow their way into every marriage. No married couple, no matter how godly, can expect to get through life without having at some point to swim in some very deep and turbulent waters. It's just part of life.

So how do you handle this? First, realize that God allows difficulties in our lives for many reasons. I'm not saying He *causes* difficulties, but He does allow them. The presence of difficulties does not mean something is wrong with your marriage.

Trials do not bring neutral results. They either drive people together or apart. The natural tendency is to go through a difficulty alone and not share it as a couple. The following are some principles we've learned:

- *Give your mate time and the freedom to process trials differently from the way you do.* Men need to avoid typical, noncompassionate responses such as: "Snap out of it, dear. Everything is going to be fine." A wife needs to resist thinking that because her husband isn't expressing the same emotions she is, he must not really care.

- *Recognize the temptation to become self-focused and to withdraw from each other.* Since it is very difficult for another person to carry your burden, there is a natural tendency to desire to pull away. As a result, you end up thinking the other person doesn't understand, and the resulting emotional pain makes you want to pull back to safety.

- *Respond to trials by embracing God's perspective of suffering as a couple.* The spouses who learn the art of facing storms together can develop a sweet and robust spiritual oneness.

- *Remember that your mate is never your enemy.* Your struggle is not against your spouse. Resist the urge to punish or think that he or she is the problem. Your spouse is your intimate ally, a fellow burden bearer who is there to encourage you as you go through a difficult time.

- *If the burden or suffering persists, seek outside help.* If you feel you are slipping into a deep ditch, find godly counsel to gain outside perspective.

Suffering afflicts all marriages; how you respond to it will determine whether your marriage flourishes or flounders.

PONDER ON YOUR OWN

Why do difficulties sometimes prompt you to see your spouse as "the enemy"? How can you resist this temptation?

DISCUSS WITH YOUR SPOUSE

■ How have you dealt so far with "deep and turbulent waters"? What have you done well? What could use some improvement? How can you get better prepared for the next difficulty that strikes?

■ Think of a time when suffering helped you grow spiritually. What happened? How can you better help each other in times of difficulty to deepen your walk with God?

STUDY WITH YOUR GROUP

■ What outside assistance has helped you the most in getting through difficult times? Discuss as much as you feel willing to share.

2. Read John 15:1–17

Would you like your marriage to blossom and grow and become a great blessing to everyone your relationship touches? If so, then you need to learn something about pruning.

Jesus made it very clear that one prerequisite of bearing fruit in the Christian life is the painful process of pruning, in which the Father cuts away what is useless or hinders us from bearing fruit. He said, "Every branch that bears fruit He prunes, that it may bear more fruit" (15:2). Just as there are laws of nature, like gravity, so it is in the spiritual realm: pruning precedes fruit bearing. God lovingly orders events, circumstances, and relationships to help us become more like Jesus Christ.

Personal godliness is God's primary goal for each of us. And while His pruning can seem severe—even too painful to bear—it is necessary, for without that pruning, we will bear little fruit.

One of the great privileges of marriage is that we do not have to go through these pruning periods alone. Through marriage, God has provided you a partner with whom you can share the pain of the pruning process.

PONDER ON YOUR OWN

- If your mate is in the midst of a season of pruning, how can you come alongside and gently remind him or her of the hope of becoming more Christlike through the suffering? If he or she is not in such a season, how can you prepare yourself for one?

DISCUSS WITH YOUR SPOUSE

- Recall with one another some times when you believe God was at work pruning you. What happened? What was the result?

STUDY WITH YOUR GROUP

- How can you identify times of divine pruning? Is hardship synonymous with pruning? Where does Hebrews 12:5–13 fit in with this discussion? How can you, as a group, apply verses 12 and 13 to this process?

- What has God done in your life through times of pruning?

KEEP ROMANCE ALIVE

1. Read Proverbs 5:18, 19

Romance is the sugar and spice of marriage. It is the fire in the fireplace—the warm response of one spouse to another that says, "We may have struggles, but I love you, and everything is okay." We can enjoy the warmth of our love for one another, even in the midst of the chilling winds of difficult times.

Romance should be a part of our everyday marriage experience. Proverbs 5:19 tells husbands to be "enraptured" with their mates. This type of powerful romance is part of what sets a marriage apart from a mere friendship. Barbara is my friend, but a side of our relationship goes way beyond that. We share a marriage bed, with intimacies reserved only for us.

God designed marriage to help you feel exhilarated with your most intimate of friends, your spouse. Don't settle for less.

PONDER ON YOUR OWN

■ Do you consider yourself a romantic person? Explain.

■ How do you and your spouse differ on the way you perceive romance? How have you responded to these differences?

DISCUSS WITH YOUR SPOUSE

■ Plan an evening of romance together. How can you include surprise as part of the festivities? How can you make romance a more regular part of your relationship?

STUDY WITH YOUR GROUP

■ Describe (as much as you can) the best romantic times you have enjoyed with your mate. Spend some time giving each other several good, creative ideas for expanding your romantic repertoire.

2. Read Song of Solomon 2:8–14

Romantic love is part of God's character. Just as He woos us to follow Him and express our love for Him, so a husband and wife should strive to win each other's affections.

Some time ago we surveyed eight hundred people at our Weekend To Remember marriage conferences. Here is our top 10 list, in reverse order, of what communicates romantic love to women:

10. *Holding hands.*

9. *Massage.* No strings attached!

8. *Acts of service and sacrifice.* Make her feel special.

7. *A kiss.*

6. *Taking a walk together.*

5. *Written notes, letters or cards.*

4. *Going out on a date.* Time away, with no kids.

3. *Having special meals together.* Candlelight helps.

2. *Touch.* Hugs, cuddles, and caresses—*without* expectation of a later payoff.

1. *Flowers.*

Ladies, show your husband the following list of male needs and ask him to prioritize them in order of importance.

1. Respect and celebrate who he is as a man and how God made him sexually.

2. Make his romantic needs (both frequency and creativity) a priority.

3. Desire him and make him feel wanted; feel unashamed of her passion for him.

4. Be adventuresome, fun, sexually imaginative, and unafraid about using her sexual power as a woman.

5. Let him know that he is a great lover, that he brings his wife great pleasure.

As Barbara and I look back on the times of passion and romance and love that we have most enjoyed, we see that most involved both special plans *and* the element of surprise . . . anything that sparked the imagination and built a sense of anticipation. It's one of the greatest secrets to keeping the romantic fires burning.

PONDER ON YOUR OWN

■ Which of the suggestions listed above are you good at with your spouse? At which are you a little weak?

DISCUSS WITH YOUR SPOUSE

■ Discuss both lists above. What do you learn about each other's needs and desires?

■ Which side of the romance equation are you better at as a couple, planning or surprise? How can you more effectively bring the other side into your experience?

STUDY WITH YOUR GROUP

■ What other activities or items, not on these lists, say to you, "I love you"? What activities or items on the list do *not* say "I love you"?

THE COMPLEMENTARY RESPONSIBILITIES OF HUSBANDS AND WIVES

THE BUSINESS WORLD has all kinds of partnerships: silent partners, financial partners, equal partners, controlling partners, minority partners, and more. But in marriage, God intended for us to have only one kind: a fully participating partnership.

The apostle Peter set forth the concept of mutual partnership when he instructed men to treat their wives as "heirs together of the grace of life" (1 Peter 3:7). Although a wife's function and role differ from that of her husband, she has an equal inheritance as a child of God. There are no inferiors or superiors in marriage.

Nevertheless, the Scriptures provide a clear organizational structure for marriage: "But I want you to know that the head of every man is Christ, the head of woman is man, and the head of Christ is God" (1 Cor. 11:3). The word *head* does not imply male dominance, where a man lords it over a woman and demands her total obedience.

God's Word clearly states that we are all equally His children and of equal value and worth (Gal. 3:28)—and yet husbands and wives have differing responsibilities within marriage.

THE COUPLE'S RESPONSIBILITIES

1. Read Genesis 2:18

Adam may have lived in the middle of a perfect garden, but he was alone. God took a look at Adam's situation and declared, "It is not good that man should be alone; I will make him a helper comparable to him." God created Eve to be Adam's companion and helper comparable to him, thus revealing one major purpose for marriage: for one spouse to complete the other.

The apostle Paul echoed this teaching when he wrote, "Nevertheless, neither is man independent of woman, nor woman independent of man, in the Lord" (1 Cor. 11:11). We really *do* need each other! As William Barclay's *New Daily Study Bible* puts it, "In the Lord, woman is nothing without man nor man without woman."[1]

Did you see the original *Rocky* film, before Sylvester Stallone started spinning off sequels? One major subplot detailed the love relationship of Rocky and Adrian. She is a little wallflower who works in the pet shop, the sister of Paulie, an insensitive goon who works at the meat house and wants to become a debt collector for a loan shark. Paulie feels suspicious of Rocky's intentions toward Adrian. He asks the fighter one day, "What's the attraction? I don't see it."

I doubt that Sylvester Stallone, who wrote the script, has any idea that his words perfectly exemplify the principle for a suitable helper described in Genesis 2. Rocky declares, "I dunno—she fills gaps."

Paulie bristles. "What gaps?" he asks.

"She got gaps; I got gaps—together we fill the gaps."[2]

In his simple but profound way, Rocky hit upon a great truth. He meant that without him, Adrian has empty places in her life; and without her, he has empty places in his. But when the two of them get together, they fill those blank spots in one another.

That's exactly what God did when He fashioned a helpmate suitable for Adam. She filled his empty places, and he filled hers.

I've never had any doubt that I need Barbara. I know she fills my gaps. I need her because she tells me the truth about myself, both the good, the bad, and the otherwise. I need Barbara to add a different perspective of life, of relationships, and of people. She also adds variety and spice to my life. She's an artist; I am not. Her pace is slower than mine. She helps me pull back on the throttle and enjoy life. She has encouraged me, for instance, to read more—and I now actually *enjoy* it. That's what a helpmate does!

PONDER ON YOUR OWN

What kinds of "empty places" do you see your spouse filling for you?

How does your spouse differ from you? How do you think those differences help make him or her a perfect complement to you?

DISCUSS WITH YOUR SPOUSE

What specific steps can you take together to better fill one another's empty spaces?

STUDY WITH YOUR GROUP

In what specific ways does God intend for men and women to complete one another? What does this plan tell you about how you are to approach your marriage and treat your spouse?

2. Read Ecclesiastes 4:9, 10

Ecclesiastes 4:9, 10 shouts the value of accountability in marriage. Consider a few areas where Barbara and I have learned to practice accountability in our own marriage:

1. *Spiritual health.* In order to remain on track, every marriage must involve daily communication with and dependence on God. A loving spouse who has permission to encourage us in our devotion to Christ can help by asking open-ended questions such as, "What has God been teaching you lately?"

2. *Emotional and sexual fidelity.* The way you handle the issues of temptation and moral struggle will largely chart the course for your relationship. Neither you nor your spouse can risk opening the door to inappropriate intimacy with someone of the opposite sex. Be open and honest about your temptations.

3. *Schedules.* We try to help each other make good decisions by monitoring each other's workload and schedules. Making good decisions means saying yes to some good things and no to others. Schedules are ultimately a statement of our *true* priorities.

4. *Money and values.* Nothing in our marriage created the need for accountability more than the checkbook! I recall some early accountability tests. Would I listen to her? Would I consider her advice? Would she trust me with a final decision? These all gave us natural opportunities to practice godly, caring accountability in each other's life.

5. *Parenting practice.* When Barbara and I had our first child, we began the lifelong process of being accountable to each other for our performance as parents. When Barbara and I noticed a good or bad tendency, we would either encourage or help the other improve.

6. *No secrets.* Secrets are one of Satan's primary tools to divide couples. Accountability between husband and wife is a superb way to keep them from messing with your marriage.

PONDER ON YOUR OWN

■ What do you think keeps you from making yourself fully accountable to your spouse? Fear of rejection? Fear of hurting him or her? Simple pride?

DISCUSS WITH YOUR SPOUSE

■ Sit down together and make a list of areas in your lives where you believer you need to be more accountable to one another. What areas do you think you both need to work on?

STUDY WITH YOUR GROUP

■ As a group, take some time to brainstorm on how married couples should be accountable to one another. How can accountability in these areas improve your marriages?

■ Should married couples keep no secrets from one another? Why do you think Satan wants to make sure husbands and wives keep secrets from one another? How does keeping secrets affect a marriage?

THE HUSBAND'S RESPONSIBILITIES

1. Read Genesis 24:67

Isaac, it is said, "took Rebekah and she became his wife, *and he loved her*" (italics added). Centuries later, that's still what a wife most wants out of marriage.

A wife wants her husband to love her, to cherish and care for her, to pursue her and continue to know who she is and who she is becoming. She wants her husband to seek a relationship with her. She wants him to strive to understand her. It's why on some occasions, our wives want to be intriguing and a challenge, not easily figured out.

When a woman sees her husband denying himself for her, she understands that it's because of love. On the other hand, if a woman senses her husband is romancing her to meet his own personal needs, then she feels manipulated, less valued . . . used. She may fear that she is being taken advantage of, taken for granted sexually, and unappreciated in all kinds of ways.

A wife's ultimate need is to be loved. No man will do that perfectly. But a husband seeking to become the man God wants him to be will learn how to better love his mate. The result is a wife who begins to feel and experience unconditional love—and a marriage of growing commitment, trust, and fulfillment.

PONDER ON YOUR OWN

■ In what specific areas do you as the husband need to more completely deny yourself—your own desires and needs—so that you can begin to better focus on what your wife needs?

Your wife wants more than anything for you to love, cherish, care for, pursue her, and understand her. How would you grade yourself in each of these areas? What can you do to make improvements in the areas that need them?

DISCUSS WITH YOUR SPOUSE

Take some time as a couple to talk about what the wife really needs from her husband. How can you better work together to meet those needs?

STUDY WITH YOUR GROUP

Why do husbands sometimes have a difficult time understanding their wives? What can a man do to better understand his mate?

2. Read John 13:1–17

Scores of books are only too willing to give you all sorts of answers about the husband's role in the home. But when you carefully analyze the biblical record, you arrive at a clear definition: the husband's role is servant-leader. God says the husband is to shoulder the responsibility of leadership in his home.

Paul summarized well the man's position when he wrote, "Husbands, love your wives, just as Christ also loved the church and gave Himself up for her" (Eph. 5:25). And just how did Christ love the church?

With self-denial: Jesus Christ stepped out of eternity into time and laid aside the privileges of deity. He denied himself, even to the point of death. Servant-leaders deny themselves for the good of their families.

With sacrificial action: Christ gave His life for those He loved. Husbands are called, daily, to give up their desires and die to self.

With a servant's heart: Jesus continually gave himself over to serving others. In the same way, husbands should surrender their own agendas—and their hobbies—to serve their wives and meet their needs.

Jesus didn't just *talk* about serving; He even washed His disciples' feet. I've washed Barbara's feet as a statement that I want to nourish and cherish her and meet her needs.

I've also found that there is no better way to serve your wife than to understand her needs and try to meet them. Making the effort to know specifics about her background, her favorite things, and her dreams all communicate to her, "I want to *know* you. I want to be your *soul mate*." I have yet to meet a woman who resented the loving service of a husband who took the time to communicate *that*!

PONDER ON YOUR OWN

As your wife's servant, can you name her top three needs? What worries her? What circumstances quickly empty her emotional gas tank?

Take the time to rate yourself from one to five in three categories: leading, loving, and serving. Then pray that you will have the courage to lead, the sensitivity to love, and the humility to serve your wife.

DISCUSS WITH YOUR SPOUSE

What practical deeds would best communicate a husband's self-sacrificing, serving love for his wife?

STUDY WITH YOUR GROUP

■ Why is it important for a woman to know that her husband cares about what she is *feeling*? Why is it important for the man to understand what his wife is feeling? How can a husband best communicate to his wife the desire to know her, to truly be her *soul mate*?

3. Read Proverbs 4:1, 2

It is Dad's job as the family minister-shepherd to bear the weight of transferring God's truth to his children. Children need their father to lead them spiritually.

Dad, you can take advantage of daily opportunities to equip your children spiritually. First, get clearly in your mind what you want to teach your children. Early in my own children's lives, I started carrying around a list I called "Twenty-five Things I Am Teaching My Kids." On this page, I listed things such as "Being faithful in little things" and "Becoming a man of character." It reminded me of what is important, beyond my daily tasks.

Over the years, that list grew to more than fifty items! I still carry the list with me, even though our children are grown. I'm still learning important lessons that I can pass along to my adult children, not as a parent, but as an adult peer.

God designed the family to be a spiritual garden. It is the single most important place where faith gets planted and hope is nurtured.

PONDER ON YOUR OWN

■ How would you rate your spiritual leadership? How can you improve your performance as your family's minister-shepherd?

DISCUSS WITH YOUR SPOUSE

■ What kinds of spiritual truths and godly principles do you want to teach your children? Write them down . . . and add to the list when either or both of you think of something new.

■ How can the two of you best work in cooperation to make sure your home is a "spiritual garden" where your children are nurtured in the faith and in godly living?

STUDY WITH YOUR GROUP

■ How specifically should fathers lead their children spiritually? What can they do in their homes and marriages to make sure their children receive training and instruction in important spiritual truths and principles? What are some of the obstacles that fathers face in leading their children spiritually? How can you overcome these obstacles?

THE WIFE'S RESPONSIBILITIES

1. Read Ephesians 5:33

An important part of God's instruction to wives is found in Ephesians 5:33, "Let the wife see that she respects her husband." Why does God focus so strongly on respect? Why didn't He select other positive and necessary traits, such as kindness, sympathy, and forgiveness? Why not emphasize love?

I believe that God, as the designer of men, knew that our husbands would be built up as we respect them. When a wife respects her husband, he feels it, receives support from it, and is strengthened by it. A man needs respect like a woman needs love.

Your husband wants and needs to make a contribution through his life that he believes is worthy of another's respect. He needs to know that you feel he is important. Without your respect, he finds it hard to respect himself. You are his mirror. When you express your respect, he feels valuable and esteemed.

When you respect your husband, you reverence him, notice him, regard him, honor him, prefer him, and esteem him. You value his opinion, admire his wisdom and character, appreciate his commitment to you, and consider his needs and values.

Every husband wants his wife to be on his team and to coach him when necessary—but most of all, to be his cheerleader. A husband needs a wife who is behind him, believing in him, appreciating him, and cheering him on.

PONDER ON YOUR OWN

- What does it mean for you as a wife to respect your husband? What attitudes do you need to demonstrate to show him that you respect him?

DISCUSS WITH YOUR SPOUSE

- Ask your husband if there are areas in your marriage where he feels disrespected. Give him the freedom to speak honestly! Then work to make sure you show him respect in those areas.

- Talk together about how you can achieve a healthy balance of respect for your husband with the need to lovingly speak correction or even constructive criticism when it's needed.

STUDY WITH YOUR GROUP

■ Talk about the meaning of the word *respect*. What is respect, and what isn't it? What attitudes and actions on the part of wives communicate respect for their husbands? Which ones communicate disrespect?

2. Read Genesis 2:18

While all of us are called to help others—"Bear one another's burdens, and so fulfill the law of Christ" (Gal. 6:2)—the Bible places a special emphasis on this responsibility for wives. It also tells us that God specially designed women to be the kinds of helpers that make them the ideal match for men.

The very first book of God's Word tells us that part of God's plan of creation—including the creation of marriage—contained this declaration: "It is not good that man should be alone; I will make him a helper comparable to him." It is interesting to note that the Hebrew word *helper* in this passage is found hereafter in the Bible only in reference to God as He helps us. The fact that God applies this word to a wife signifies that women have been given tremendous power for good in their husbands' lives.

This remarkable verse tells us that God has designed wives to be very much like their husbands—comparable—but also different in ways that complement or help their husbands become all that God intends them to be.

PONDER ON YOUR OWN

■ What do you think it means to be your husband's "helper?" How does this differ from the role of a subordinate?

In what ways are you different from your husband—especially those ways that make you a complement to him?

DISCUSS WITH YOUR SPOUSE

Talk about the burdens your husband must bear—make a list. Then discuss how you can better help to bear your husband's burdens.

STUDY WITH YOUR GROUP

Why do you think God created wives to be different in so many ways from their husbands? Why not just make them completely alike? What does that tell you about God's plan for marriage?

3. Read Leviticus 19:3

God has uniquely designed women to be mothers, and the greatest way a mother can love her children is to love their father. The Bible teaches that God has created a woman with an innate and special ability to nurture and care for her family.

Therefore, mothers are the primary people whom God designed to love, nurture, and mentor children. Without question, this is one of the reasons why God so often insists that children are to honor their mothers.

We believe these crucial responsibilities of nurturing and caring for children should be met before a mother contemplates *any* other duties. This is more difficult today than it was a few decades ago, because our culture has seriously devalued the role of a mother. Nevertheless, we ought to elevate motherhood to its rightfully high place by pointing out its exalted value in God's economy of the family.

Let us encourage mothers to model love for God and His Word, to love their husbands, and to love their children. It's what they were designed for.

PONDER ON YOUR OWN

■ How can a wife effectively model the importance of motherhood and give it its rightfully high place in God's plan?

DISCUSS WITH YOUR SPOUSE

■ What important roles do you as a couple see for the mother in a family? How can your husband assist and support you in fulfilling those roles?

■ Take a pen and pad and write down the things you and your husband can do to teach your children the importance of honoring their mother. (Dad, don't forget that it's your job to *model* those things in your own words and actions.)

STUDY WITH YOUR GROUP

■ In what ways has God clearly designed mothers to be their children's primary source of love, nurturing, and mentoring? In what ways has our culture devalued or downplayed the importance of motherhood? What can we as Christians do to elevate motherhood to its rightful place?

LIVING BY FAITH

FAR TOO MANY BELIEVERS TODAY feel impotent to make a difference in their own homes, much less in their communities. The battlefront is so vast and the problems so overwhelming that many have determined that our nation cannot be redeemed.

Such pessimism betrays a lack of faith in the power of God. A follower of Christ controlled by unbelief will almost never see God work in and through his life. Unbelief caused nearly an entire generation of Israelites to perish in the wilderness. As the writer of Hebrews says, "So we see that they could not enter in because of unbelief" (3:19). They simply didn't believe God could overcome the giants they saw in their way.

Unbelief begins with dangerous assumptions and concludes that some problem is too big for God, that God doesn't want to act on our behalf, and that we might as well eat, drink, and be merry, for tomorrow we die (1 Cor. 15:32). Unbelief gives birth to a mundane Christian life that knows little of the supernatural working of God—the ultimate waste, a life of mediocrity.

Don't give in to it! Learn to take small steps of faith by choosing to believe God's Word and acting on that belief, whether you feel like it or not. Keep in mind the words of Martin Luther: "Feelings come and feelings go, and feelings are deceiving; my warrant is the Word of God, naught else is worth believing."

1. Read Hebrews 11:1

Faith is an invisible but active ingredient in every spiritually growing marriage. It's the catalyst that causes you to implement biblical principles in your relationship, trusting God to use your obedience to build oneness.

Many people, however, would find it difficult to give a true biblical definition of faith. Some people use the word almost as a substitute for belief, as in, "I am part of the Christian faith, while my neighbor is part of the Muslim faith."

I like the definition of faith provided by Ney Bailey in her book *Faith Is Not a Feeling*: "Faith is taking God at His word. . . . God's Word is truer than anything I feel. God's Word is truer than anything I experience. God's Word is truer than any circumstances I will ever face. God's Word is truer than anything in the world."[1] That's what the writer of Hebrews means when he describes faith as "the substance of things hoped for, the evidence of things not seen" (11:1).

The object of our faith is God and His Word. You must place your trust in what God has said. But if you don't know what He has said in His Word, how can you believe? That's why Paul told the Romans, "Faith comes by hearing, and hearing by the word of God" (Rom. 10:17).

PONDER ON YOUR OWN

In your opinion, how do belief and faith differ? What does the Bible mean by "trust"?

DISCUSS WITH YOUR SPOUSE

What are you trusting God for that only He can do in your marriage? Ask God to increase your faith and enable you to grow closer to Him and to each another.

What promises of God as declared in Scripture mean the most to you? Why?

STUDY WITH YOUR GROUP

▨ Discuss Ney Bailey's definition of faith. How do you react to this definition? What would you add? Alter? Why?

2. Read 1 Chronicles 29:11

A friend of mine gave me a customized, framed quote for my office. I guess he must have felt I needed it. It read:

Dennis:

Trust Me. I have everything under control.

Jesus

I've read that quote on more than one occasion when I needed to be reminded of the truth—He is in control. In fact, nothing happens in our lives apart from what God allows or ordains.

Yet this same sovereign Lord seeks a close relationship with us. As the following two passages tell us, He is our Comforter during times of distress and suffering:

• "The Lord is near to the brokenhearted and saves those who are crushed in spirit" (Ps. 34:18 NASB).

• "Fear not, for I am with you, be not dismayed, for I am your God; I will strengthen you, I will help you, I will uphold you with my victorious right hand" (Isa. 41:10 RSV).

When you remember Who is in control, you will realize that your life is never really out of control. And that is why you can step out in faith, trusting in a sovereign God.

PONDER ON YOUR OWN

▨ What does it mean to you that God is "sovereign"? Does this knowledge help you to step out in faith? Why or why not?

DISCUSS WITH YOUR SPOUSE

▨ What areas of your married life have sometimes seemed out of control? Why? How can you reconcile these times with belief in a sovereign God?

▨ How can you help each other to remember and live—especially in difficult times—according to the truth of a sovereign God?

STUDY WITH YOUR GROUP

▨ Discuss the following quote: "Nothing happens in our lives apart from what God allows or ordains." Do you agree? Why? What difference does such a belief make in day-to-day living?

3. Read John 14:16

Most Christians agree that the Holy Spirit is the third person of the Trinity. When I was a little boy growing up in a church that used only the King James Version, we referred to Him as the Holy Ghost. And for a long time I could imagine only something like the cartoon character Casper the Friendly Ghost, floating through walls like a puff of smoke. The Holy Ghost was not someone that I could relate to as a boy. I am glad today that He is usually referred to as the Holy Spirit.

For years I referred to the Holy Ghost as "it." But the Holy Spirit Jesus describes is a person, sent not only to glorify Christ, but also to be our Counselor, Advisor, Advocate, Defender, Director, Guide, and Helper who will "abide with you forever."

If you are interested in living the abundant life Jesus promised, then you must rightly relate to the Holy Spirit. Just think of all the sermons you've heard on the Christian life, all the books you've read about marriage. If you try in your own power to obey God and follow all that advice, you may have short-term success, but over time you will fail . . . period. It's impossible. You need God's power, which is available to you as you yield moment by moment to the Holy Spirit, sent to us by Christ to empower us to live the Christian life.

PONDER ON YOUR OWN

■ What picture do you have of the Holy Spirit? How has your understanding changed as you have grown older?

DISCUSS WITH YOUR SPOUSE

■ How can you help one another tap into the power of the Holy Spirit?

■ Do you believe you and your family are enjoying the "abundant life" Jesus promised through the power of the Holy Spirit? Explain. How can you start enjoying more of that promised life?

STUDY WITH YOUR GROUP

■ Discuss the various roles or activities of the Holy Spirit: Counselor, Advisor, Advocate, Defender, Director, Guide, and Helper. How have you seen the Holy Spirit functioning in your life in each of these ways?

4. Read Isaiah 27:6

Do you want to grow up in your faith? Do you and your spouse desire to know the deep joy that comes from maturing in your relationship with God? If so, I have an insider's secret that will help. For centuries followers of Jesus have recognized the critical importance of *discipline*. While I have no interest in a lifeless list of legalistic tasks that will turn the Christian life into a graceless, joyless religion based on works, I know that certain basic exercises will change a flabby, weak faith into a strong one. Consider a few of the most important:

• *Prayer*. Prayer is the way we communicate with God. Pray both as individuals and as a couple.

• *Bible study*. In God's Word we learn everything we need to know about God, His promises, and what He wants from us.

• *Worship*. Find a vibrant, Christ-worshipping, Bible-believing church, and commit to regular worship there.

• *Giving*. We own nothing; we are simply stewards of resources, on loan from God.

• *Fellowship*. We need others and they need us to accomplish the work of the kingdom.

• *Service*. Every local church needs people to use their spiritual gifts and natural abilities to serve others.

• *Witness*. Jesus has entrusted to us the task of reconciling men and women to God.

The apostle Paul instructed Timothy to exercise himself for godliness. When you practice these important spiritual disciplines, you'll be getting the kind of workout that makes you spiritually strong.

PONDER ON YOUR OWN

Could you make use of commute time or an exercise session by carrying a pocket-sized Bible or listening to the Bible on CD or your MP3 player?

DISCUSS WITH YOUR SPOUSE

What are the possibilities of the two of you regularly praying together briefly before you go to sleep at night?

STUDY WITH YOUR GROUP

How can you effectively build strong relationships within your group? Could you offer to lead a small group Bible study at your church? What ministries in your community need volunteers to feed the hungry and help the poor? Seek one out!

■ How can you cultivate friendships with neighbors, plant seeds by sharing your testimony along with insights from God's Word, and extend an invitation for them to receive Christ? How can you let the light of Jesus shine out of your life?

5. Read Mark 1:35

Early in the gospel of Mark, we read how Jesus handled the stress of ministering to hundreds of needy people: "Now in the morning, having risen a long while before daylight, He went out and departed to a solitary place; and there He prayed."

Being a spouse and a parent carries many inherent pressures, and many individuals find it easy to make alone time with God the first casualty of a busy day. But if Jesus, who probably handled more stress before breakfast than any of us handle in a week, made the time to get alone and pray, then we have no excuse for not doing the same thing. If He did it, we should too.

We are big advocates of couples praying together, but as important as that is, it is just as important for husbands and wives to find their own time to be *absolutely alone* with God.

PONDER ON YOUR OWN

■ What do you think is so important about spending regular time alone with God? How have you benefited from such time?

DISCUSS WITH YOUR SPOUSE

■ How can you help each other find and make time to get alone with God? How might you make this part of your accountability to one another?

■ Who do you know that has a high quality devotional time with God? How does it shape his or her life? What can you learn from this person about improving your own time alone with God?

STUDY WITH YOUR GROUP

■ Describe what your individual times with God look like. What do you do? Where do you have these devotional meeting times? How long do they generally last? What fruit have you seen come from them?

6. Read Job 1:6

Each of us lives in the middle of an unseen spiritual world. Just as God is accomplishing His work on earth, so Satan is seeking to undermine God's work in you and your mate.

That is precisely what the devil had in mind when he brought Job to God's attention. He intended to destroy this righteous man's faith and prove that no one would follow God unless he enjoyed an unending stream of physical blessings.

Centuries later Peter wrote, "Be sober, be vigilant; because your adversary the devil walks about like a roaring lion, seeking whom he may devour" (1 Peter 5:8). Lions prey upon the weak, the unsuspecting, the unprotected, and the stragglers. Similarly, Satan looks for marriages with weak spots, mates with unprotected self-esteem issues, and spouses who live independently of each other. Be advised, and be on the alert.

"Be strong in the Lord and in the power of His might," Paul wrote. "Put on the whole armor of God, that you may be able to stand against the wiles of the devil" (Eph. 6:10, 11). Standing firm in Christ means living obediently and believing that what God says is true, regardless of how you feel.

PONDER ON YOUR OWN

■ What do you believe about the devil? What have you experienced of spiritual warfare?

DISCUSS WITH YOUR SPOUSE

■ Where is Satan most attacking your marriage right now? What kind of help do you need in thwarting these satanic attacks? Be specific.

■ How have you responded in the past when your marriage and family have taken a "hit" from the enemy? How can you better prepare for the satanic attacks that are surely coming your way? Be specific.

STUDY WITH YOUR GROUP

■ Discuss the following quote: "Lions prey upon the weak, the unsuspecting, the unprotected, and the stragglers. Similarly, Satan looks for marriages with weak spots, mates with unprotected self-esteem issues, and spouses who live independently of each other." Do you see yourself in any of these descriptions? How can you help each other prepare for the assaults of the devil?

7. Read 1 Kings 19:2, 3

The enemy of our souls likes us to remain isolated. He wants us to make major decisions—like choosing a mate or a vocation—without asking for the counsel of other mature believers.

If you do not appreciate the vulnerability of isolation, then let me point to some memorable biblical examples. Each of these men was alone when Satan tempted him:

- Joseph was alone when Potiphar's wife propositioned him.

- David was alone as he gawked at Bathsheba.

- Peter was alone when he denied Christ.

Elijah was also alone after he'd won a great victory over the prophets of Baal, and in his isolation, a wicked queen froze his heart with a deadly threat. He actually ran away—the same man who earlier had called down fire from heaven on his adversaries! (See 2 Kings 1:10, 12.) He even asked to resign from active prophetic duty. God responded by telling him, "I have reserved seven thousand in Israel, all whose knees have not bowed to Baal" (1 Kings 19:18). Elijah was not alone at all, but as long as he remained isolated, he caved in to depression.

Don't remain isolated! It's not a safe place to be. Instead, seek wise counsel from other godly men and women who can give you perspective and courage when you need it most.

PONDER ON YOUR OWN

Describe a time when isolation made you a special target for Satan. What happened?

DISCUSS WITH YOUR SPOUSE

Are you in any way isolated emotionally, spiritually, or physically from your spouse? If so, what can you do to draw near and become one?

■ What mature believers in your life can offer you important counsel? How often do you avail yourselves of their counsel? Explain.

STUDY WITH YOUR GROUP

■ Is it possible to feel isolated even in a group? Explain. How can you try to make sure that your times together do not deepen anyone's isolation?

8. Read Exodus 34:21

One of the most profound and powerful principles in all of Scripture is that *spiritual rest precedes spiritual growth.* That's part of what the Sabbath is all about.

God knows that after six days of work, everyone needs a break. That's why He commanded, "Six days you shall work, but on the seventh day you shall rest." That's the reason for the Sabbath—to give us regularly scheduled time to relax, reflect, think critically about life, and find a time of peace where we can clearly hear the voice of our Father. This is when parents can regroup and refocus on what needs to happen spiritually in their own lives and within their family.

When we yield control of our lives to the Father—when we take a day to turn from our activity in order to abide more fully in Him—we receive strength for daily living throughout the coming week. You might say a Sabbath rest is like a weekly tune-up for your soul.

PONDER ON YOUR OWN

▓ How can you use one day each week to regroup and refocus on what needs to happen spiritually in your life and within your family. Are you taking advantage of such a day? Why or why not?

▓ Is a Sabbath rest like a weekly tune-up for your own soul? Explain.

DISCUSS WITH YOUR SPOUSE

▓ Is Sunday any different from the other days of the week for you and your family? If so, how? If not, in what ways are you missing out not only on physical refreshment, but also on spiritual restoration?

STUDY WITH YOUR GROUP

▓ Of the reasons listed for the existence of the Sabbath—to give us regularly scheduled time to relax, reflect, think critically about life, and find a time of peace where we can clearly hear the voice of our Father—which is most significant for you? What other reasons can you give for taking one day off a week to rest? How do you best rest?

9. Read Isaiah 26:3

A battle rages within each of us, especially those who attempt to build godly marriages and families in a culture that stands against nearly everything God has to say about love, marriage, and family. It's a battle to overcome fear with faith.

The phrase "fear not" appears 365 times in the Bible. Like a daily vitamin, God has provided just what we need to conquer our daily dreads. Faith in Jesus Christ and the promises of His Word will cause fear to flee. Instead of feeling terrorized, paralyzed, and hypnotized by our fears, faith galvanizes our character with courage.

The world sees fear and anxiety as normal, but God's Word tells us to allow His peace to take up residence in our hearts: "You will keep him in perfect peace, whose mind is stayed on You, because he trusts in You." Notice the sequence: *We* put our trust in God; *we* focus on the truth of God and His Word; and *He* keeps us in "perfect peace."

Fear makes us fret about what lies ahead, but faith calls us to cast all our cares upon our heavenly Father. Faith trumps fear . . . so long as it's faith in Almighty God. Those who do put their faith in God—who make their faith a way of thinking, acting, and being—get to live and walk in God's peace. And that's the only perfect peace any of us can ever know.

PONDER ON YOUR OWN

How do you deal with the fear of "What if?"? How does fear urge you to worry about tomorrow?

DISCUSS WITH YOUR SPOUSE

How do you deal with the following common fears: whether your husband will ever become the spiritual leader in your marriage and family; a child who is not making wise choices; resolving debt and paying the bills; health issues; caring for aging parents?

STUDY WITH YOUR GROUP

■ How does faith trump fear? How has it trumped fear in your own experience?

■ In what circumstances does your faith threaten to get overwhelmed? Who and what can you count on in such times to overcome fear?

10. Read Numbers 13:30

My heart resonates with Caleb. I want to be like him! He once declared, "Let us go up at once and take possession [of the promised land], for we are well able to overcome it." Caleb believed the promises of God and called the nation of Israel to take a step of faith.

I'm so convinced of the validity of God's promises in Scripture that I will make this offer: I will renounce Christianity if any person can show me a better system on which to base my life. I have challenged hundreds with that offer, yet no one has even suggested an alternative. It's not hard to see why. *There are none.*

Since I gave my life to Christ in 1969, I've attempted to live my life based on what I know to be true. Here are some of those bedrock truths:

- Walking with God is an electrifying adventure.

- A life of faith brings a genuine and lasting sense of destiny and significance.

- It is a wonderful privilege to be used by God for His eternal purposes.

- God's Holy Spirit empowers me to deny my selfishness and enables me to love people (some of whom I don't even like).

- When I obey God and walk with Him, I enjoy a sense of peace, well-being, and contentment.

Be like Caleb! Step out and call your family to join you in the adventure of walking with God and being used by Him for His thrilling purposes.

PONDER ON YOUR OWN

In what area of your life do you need to believe God's Word and take a step of faith today?

DISCUSS WITH YOUR SPOUSE

How can you make your home a place more ready for an adventure of faith? What risks could you take for Christ?

How do you think God might want to use you and your family for His purposes . . . if you could only step out in faith? What would it take to make that step of faith?

STUDY WITH YOUR GROUP

On what bedrock truths do you base your life? Do they help you live an adventure in faith? Why or why not?

EMBRACING A SENSE OF MISSION

JUST BEFORE THE PATRIARCH JACOB DIED, he gathered his sons around him to deliver a stunning prophecy about their futures. He wanted them to know that God had created them all for a purpose.

"For we are His workmanship," Paul wrote in a similar vein, "created in Christ Jesus for good works, which God prepared beforehand that we should walk in them" (Eph. 2:10).

One of the most important things we need to know—and teach our children—is that God has a plan for each of us, and that we can obediently and purposefully walk in the center of that plan. God has given each of us unique abilities, personality traits, and other qualities to help us fulfill his unique plan.

No matter where you end up professionally or vocationally, God can use your talents and gifts to further His kingdom. God has a unique and special mission for each of his children—and the most fulfilling and blessed pursuit for every believer is obediently and enthusiastically living in a way that fulfills that mission.

1. Read Genesis 1:26, 27

God's first purpose for creating man and woman and joining them in marriage was to mirror His image on planet Earth. Focus your attention on those words: *mirror His image*. The Hebrew word for *mirror* means "to reflect, to magnify, exalt, and glorify."

God intends for *your* marriage to reflect His image to a world that desperately needs to see who He is. That's why your mirror needs constant polishing in the light of His Word. Because *you* are created in the image of God, people who wouldn't otherwise know what God is like should be able to look at you and your relationship with your spouse and get a genuine, awe-inspiring glimpse of the divine.

PONDER ON YOUR OWN

How does your life magnify, exalt, and glorify God? In what areas of your life do you most struggle to glorify God? What one thing would most help you follow Christ's lordship in these areas?

DISCUSS WITH YOUR SPOUSE

How does your marriage magnify, exalt, and glorify God? In what areas of your marriage do you most struggle to glorify God? What one thing would most help you follow Christ's lordship in these areas?

When the world views your marriage, can God's image be clearly seen? How are you using God's Word to "polish" your mirror? What are you willing to change in your life in order to give others an "awe-inspiring glimpse of the divine"?

STUDY WITH YOUR GROUP

▣ When people look at you and your relationship with your spouse, do they get a genuine, awe-inspiring glimpse of the divine? Explain.

2. Read Genesis 5:1–32

Too many couples raise their children without a sense of mission and direction. They never evaluate their lives in light of the Great Commission (Matt. 28:18–20). But God's original plan called for the home to be a sort of greenhouse, a nurturing place where children learn godly character, values, and integrity.

Your assignment is to impart a sense of destiny to your children, to make your home a place where your children learn what it means to love and obey God. Your home should be a training center to equip your children to meet the needs of people and the world, even as Jesus did. If children do not embrace this spiritual mission as they grow up, they may live their entire lives without the privilege of God using them in a significant way.

Your marriage is far more important than you may have imagined. It affects God's reputation on this planet! A line of godly descendants—your children—will carry a reflection of God's character to the next generation, just as it did at the very beginning.

PONDER ON YOUR OWN

▣ How have you tried to impart a sense of destiny to your children? What attempts have you made to create a home in which your children can learn what it means to love and obey God?

■ Have you ever considered inviting a missionary home on furlough to stay in your home for a few days, or at least to come and tell your family about his or her work? If not, why not start those discussions today?

DISCUSS WITH YOUR SPOUSE

■ How can you help your children, at whatever their stage of development, gain a sense of divine mission? How can you give them "practice" for their lives as adults?

STUDY WITH YOUR GROUP

■ How do you think your marriage affects God's reputation on this planet? How has it done so already? How could it do so in the future?

3. Read Psalm 126:1–3

Every godly vision is fueled by what could and should be. It is an earnest quest for God's alternative, a desire to fulfill what He wants to accomplish in and through your lives, marriage, and family. Furthermore, a godly vision for your life will rock boats—our Savior was crucified because He shook up the system.

Does your family have a vision that will affect the present and the eternal? Are you teaching your children that they have a divinely ordered destiny? Are you adding fuel to their dreams and visions by encouraging their faith and steps of courage? Are you helping them see the eternal in the midst of time?

Do you want your family to follow you? Remember, no one follows an insignificant person with trivial goals.

PONDER ON YOUR OWN

■ When you dream, do you dream about the things of God, the truly permanent? Or do you fantasize about the things of the world, the truly perishable?

■ What injustice causes you to pound the table and weep?

DISCUSS WITH YOUR SPOUSE

■ Where do you believe God is directing you to go with your marriage and family? How do you believe God wants you to reach the place where He's calling you?

STUDY WITH YOUR GROUP

■ What kind of godly vision for your life and family will "rock boats"? Who that you know has a family vision that rocks boats? What is this vision? Why does it rock boats? What's good about questioning the status quo?

4. Read Ecclesiastes 1:1–2:26

As you travel through life, do you sometimes find yourself stuck in some deeply dug ruts? In the book of Ecclesiastes, Solomon challenges us to examine our ruts and realize the impact they have on us and on those around us. He wants us to stop, climb out of the ruts, and consider carefully where we're headed. He dares us to *think* about God and His purposes for our lives.

In the first two chapters, Solomon reflects on all the ways he has tried to seek satisfaction. He looked for life in knowledge and intelligence (1:12–18), in sensual pleasure (2:1–3), in a strong work ethic (2:4), in hobbies (2:5, 6), in possessions (2:7, 8), and in a lofty life position (2:9). All of it counted for precisely *nothing*. Solomon called it vanity and concluded that *everything* is vanity when you leave God out.

What a conclusion to reach at the end of a celebrated life! Think of it! Years wasted in a fruitless quest for happiness, unsuccessfully trying to quench a raging thirst for significance.

But like a shaft of light breaking into Solomon's dark prison of despair come these words: "Then I turned myself to consider wisdom" (2:12). Finally, Solomon stopped *pursuing* and started *thinking*. He began to think about life from God's perspective—and once you do that, you break free from your ruts and the journey begins to make sense.

PONDER ON YOUR OWN

What "ruts" may you need to climb out of? How can you begin? What may happen if you don't?

DISCUSS WITH YOUR SPOUSE

How can you encourage one another to think deeply and biblically about your family and its spiritual future?

How often do you speak to your children about God's purposes for their lives? How can you start to do this more often and more effectively?

STUDY WITH YOUR GROUP

▨ How can you help each other become more spiritually minded? How willing are you to let others ask you if your actions, attitudes, and words please Christ? Explain.

5. Read Matthew 28:18–20

At one point in our marriage, Barbara and I had a conversation in which we found ourselves asking some vexing questions:

- *What kind of family is God calling us to be?*

- *What does He want us uniquely to do?*

- *Where do we fit into the Great Commission?*

- *How might God use our marriage to advance His work?*

As we wrestled with these questions, we discovered that we had never really hammered out our family's values *together*. We had never asked ourselves, "Where *must* we succeed? Where are we *unwilling* to fail?" We needed to look ten, twenty, even fifty years down the road and consider where we wanted to absolutely, positively win. That realization led us to our first courageous choice.

It can be yours, too.

Choose to spell out your family values together and use them to guide your future commitments of time, energy, money, and aspirations. What do you believe God has uniquely gifted you and called you to do? What kind of choices will most effectively enable you to carry out that calling?

The apostle Paul wrote that we are God's "workmanship, created in Christ Jesus for good works, which God prepared beforehand that we should walk in them" (Eph. 2:10). By understanding how God has made us—our skills and abilities, our individual personalities and passions, and our values—we can begin to see which good works God has called us to and how we can fulfill His purposes for our lives.

We discovered that understanding and embracing our own set of values based on Scripture takes the pressure off. We don't need to worry about how others are living. We don't have to waste energy looking over our shoulders. We can focus on God's direction for *our* lives.

PONDER ON YOUR OWN

How did God make you—your skills, individual personality, passions, and values? How do these give you a clue to God's direction for your life?

DISCUSS WITH YOUR SPOUSE

Where *must* you succeed as a family? What does this imply about what you should be doing right now? Where are you *unwilling* to fail as a family? What does this imply about what you should be doing right now?

What are your core family values? If you don't know, or haven't hammered them out together, begin to do so today.

STUDY WITH YOUR GROUP

As you look ten, twenty, even fifty years down the road, where do you want to absolutely, positively win? How can you get there? What might you need to change? What might you need to strengthen?

6. Read Matthew 25:14–21

When your children listen to you speak or watch you work, do they get the idea that believers in Jesus Christ should strive for excellence in everything they do? Do they see you working wholeheartedly for the Lord, and not for men? We believe this should be one of our primary tasks, to use both our words and our actions to encourage our children toward a life of excellence.

Of course, we do not mean attaining perfection or applying identical standards to every child. Rather, we propose that within their God-given capabilities, every child be challenged to rise above the crowd, to seek higher standards of achievement, and to become all that God has gifted him or her to be.

This was a real challenge, especially during the years when we had four teenagers living in our home. There's always tension between understanding a child's talent and ability and stretching him or her to attainable goals. Many times Barbara and I would pray and ask God if we were too lenient, and on other occasions we'd ask Him if we were too tough. In every situation, our dependence upon God helped us decide and trust Him with both the process and the results.

Training children to step above mediocrity also helps them reject half-heartedness in their relationship with God. Jesus pointed to a coming day when God will say to His diligent children, "Well done, good and faithful servant; you were faithful over a few things, I will make you ruler over many things" (25:21).

It is our job as parents to teach our children to be trustworthy, to fulfill their commitments, and to do a good job even when nobody is looking. In the end, they need to learn to do their work "heartily, as to the Lord" (Col. 3:23).

PONDER ON YOUR OWN

What does "excellence" mean to you? How would you define spiritual excellence? How do you know when you've achieved it?

DISCUSS WITH YOUR SPOUSE

What practical steps can you take to encourage your children to pursue a life of excellence? How can you keep this from becoming an unhealthy demand for performance?

In what ways do you see your home as "excellent"? In what ways could it move more in that direction? How do you propose to move it in that direction?

STUDY WITH YOUR GROUP

How have others encouraged you toward excellence for God and His Kingdom? Try to describe a specific incident.

7. Read Psalm 112:1–3

God calls you to live before your family according to His agenda. That means He wants you to build your life around the Great Commandment (to love God with all that you are) and the Great Commission (to preach the gospel to the world around you). Your words and actions ought to reflect these twin directives as your top priorities.

One of your assignments as parents is to impart to your family members a vision for the world. One way to do this is by making every family member a part of your own ministry (you do have one, you know). Share stories of how God is at work. Take them with you on trips and give them each a responsibility in your ministry. You and I are a part of a generational relay race in which we must make a good handoff to the next generation.

Your words can also create a godly direction for your children, prodding them toward good things. And with 6 billion people on this planet, children today desperately need a sense of mission! They *must* have a sense of God's imprint on their lives, encouraging and prompting them to do His work throughout their lives.

And here's the great news: *you* have the tremendous privilege of marking their lives with a divine imprint through your well-chosen words. Don't nag or preach—just keep on speaking truth and using your words to direct those you love into God's best. Remember, your marriage and family are the headwaters of your legacy. What occurs downstream in your ministry will be only as deep as the source at home.

PONDER ON YOUR OWN

- How would you describe your ministry? How are you encouraging your children to take part in your ministry?

DISCUSS WITH YOUR SPOUSE

- What stories can you tell your children that show how God is at work in your lives and in your world?

▓ What sense of God's imprint do your children have on their lives? What is encouraging and prompting them to do His work throughout their years on earth?

STUDY WITH YOUR GROUP

▓ How can you use your words to direct your loved ones into God's best? Imagine that you're speaking to your children; what will you say to them to give them a sense of mission?

8. Read John 8:32

Like a sea captain after a storm, who finds his ship heading in an errant direction, we may need to change course when confronted with the truth. Christ famously said, "The truth shall make you free," but as Herbert Agar wrote in *A Time for Greatness*, "The truth that makes men free is for the most part the truth which men prefer not to hear."[1]

What is the Bible to you? A collection of nice stories? The foundation of a conservative worldview? Or is it God's Word, "living and powerful, and sharper than any two-edged sword" (Heb. 4:12)? Is it your source of wisdom and truth about life? Does anything keep you from obeying God's Word in every area of your life—your business, your marriage, your family? Have you been avoiding some truth, or been unwilling to confront a particular area of your relationship? Do you need to adjust your course?

When you spend time reading and applying God's Word, you get your true bearings. Since its eternal truth doesn't change, you need to adjust your life to walk in that truth. As you do so, pray that God's Word will be your guide and your rock in establishing your personal convictions and beliefs, as well as your family values and priorities.

PONDER ON YOUR OWN

What is the Bible to you? Is it a collection of religious sayings, or a blueprint for living? How does it shape your life on a day-to-day basis?

DISCUSS WITH YOUR SPOUSE

How may you need to adjust your life to better conform to God's Word? What areas seem to need the most work? Why?

What, if anything, keeps you from obeying God's Word in every area of your life—your business, your marriage, your family? Have you been avoiding some truth, or been unwilling to confront a particular area of your marital relationship?

STUDY WITH YOUR GROUP

Take some extended time to pray that God's Word will be your guide and your rock in establishing your personal convictions and beliefs, as well as your family values and priorities.

9. Read Ezekiel 44:15, 16

God wants your family to be a light in a dark world. And make no mistake— an ordinary family really can have a tremendous impact on our world.

In the early days of World War II, a large Allied army found itself trapped in the channel port of Dunkirk. Hitler's tank forces, only miles away, were gearing up to smash forward. Britain's Royal Navy lacked the ships to mount a rescue. But then, as William Manchester described in his book *The Last Lion*, "a strange fleet appeared: trawlers and tugs, scows and fishing sloops, lifeboats and pleasure craft, smacks and coasters . . . even the London Fire Brigade's fire-float *Massey Shaw*—all of them manned by civilian volunteers: English fathers, sailing to rescue England's exhausted, bleeding sons."[2]

This ragtag civilian armada brought 338,682 men safely to the shores of England. Common people had made the difference.

Today, our nation's marriages and children face their own Dunkirk. And I wonder, *Will there be enough common people willing to set sail to rescue this generation of exhausted, bleeding children of divorce and broken families?*

The task may seem massive, given the deteriorated state of marriage and families in our culture. But like the common people who rescued the soldiers at Dunkirk, we can do our part by reaching out to those in our neighborhoods and our workplaces with the hope of the gospel and the wisdom of God's Word.

PONDER ON YOUR OWN

How can your *particular* family be a spiritual light in your *particular* world?

DISCUSS WITH YOUR SPOUSE

Do you believe that God can and will use you and your family to spiritually rescue hurting people around you? Why or why not?

■ Who in your neighborhood and workplaces needs the hope and wisdom of the gospel? How can you help to get it to them?

STUDY WITH YOUR GROUP

■ What makes "common people" do uncommon things? What will motivate you to take part in a "spiritual Dunkirk" in which you reach beyond your comfort zone to help the victims of disintegrating marriages and a callous culture?

10. Read Jonah 1:1–3

How do we determine what God wants us to do? How can we discover a genuine sense of mission for our lives and families?

1. *Pray—ask God to so burden your heart with someone or something that you can't let it go.* This process may take several months. Sometimes I think God wants us to demonstrate that we're really serious! But He will make it clear what He wants you to do.

2. *Look back over the tapestry of your life.* Do any threads show up repeatedly? God may have been preparing you for just this moment.

3. *Begin to take your idea to a few friends, starting with your mate and family.* Be careful here! Sometimes the Christian community can feel threatened by a genuine burden from the Lord. If someone has no vision for his own life or ministry, he can start to feel guilty when he hears about someone else's vision.

4. *Count the cost—and then do something about it.*

5. *Remember that it is in your best interest to obey God.* Jonah ran from God's assignment and wound up tossed overboard and in the belly of

a giant fish! Blessing comes from obeying God; chastening comes when we disobey.

God calls all of us take part in the Great Commission, going into all the world to share God's good news for humankind and to make disciples of all nations (Matt. 28:19, 20).

PONDER ON YOUR OWN

How much do you desire to discover God's calling on your life and family? What are you willing to do to make that discovery?

DISCUSS WITH YOUR SPOUSE

What are you and your family doing to share the good news with others? How do you think you fit in with the Great Commission?

What "cost" is involved in discovering God's will for your family and then putting a plan in action to accomplish it? How willing are you to pay this cost?

STUDY WITH YOUR GROUP

How can you help each other discover God's plan for your lives and families? How can you help put that plan into action? How can you encourage each other to plow ahead despite difficulties?

LEAVING A LEGACY

WE LIVE IN URGENT TIMES that present tremendous challenges to Christian parents. We need all the courage we can muster—all that God gives us—in order to raise our children to be the kind of people He calls them to be. One of the greatest needs of our day is parents willing to courageously follow Christ as they encounter opposition from the culture and raise their children to be spiritual warriors for their generation.

The Lord's words to Joshua apply to today's parents: "Do not be afraid, nor be dismayed; be strong and of good courage, for thus the Lord will do to all your enemies against whom you fight" (Josh. 10:25). God will build moral fortitude into His children, regardless of our gene pools. Courageous actions do cost us something, but encouraging words like these from our Father compel me to rise from my easy chair and march toward the action.

1. Read Deuteronomy 6

Too many of us lack a true, biblical vision for children and parenting. In Deuteronomy 6, God reveals why He commands parents to be fruitful—not merely to have children, but to raise godly children *who will pass on a godly legacy as one generation connects to the next.*

The home is the best place for a child to learn about God. In a culture of weakening character and ethics, our best hope for spiritual renewal lies in the restoration of godly homes. God created the family circle to be the supreme conductor of Christianity to children and to the next generation. If you consider yourself a Christ-following parent, then it is a big part of your God-given responsibility and privilege to raise your children in a way that leaves them desiring the kind of relationship with God that you display day in and day out. Although it's sobering to bring children into a decadent society, your children will become His agents in advancing the kingdom of God. Neil Postman reminded us of the generational power of children: "Our children are the living messengers we send to a time we will not see."[1]

Let's recapture the conviction that parenting is a sacred calling and that children are worth the effort! God has selected parents for a work the angels must envy—the stewardship of a child's soul.

PONDER ON YOUR OWN

Describe your vision for children and parenting. What do you think God wants to accomplish through your family?

DISCUSS WITH YOUR SPOUSE

What does it mean to the two of you that parenting is a "sacred calling"? How does this change the way you raise your children?

What are your children learning about God from you? What are they learning from your words? From your actions? From your priorities? From your friendships? From your attitude?

STUDY WITH YOUR GROUP

▨ Discuss Postman's comment: "Our children are the living messengers we send to a time we will not see." What messages will your children be sending to the future? What messages do you want them to send? How can you improve your chances that the two will match?

2. Read Psalm 112:1, 2

One primary reason why God established marriage was so that people could leave a godly legacy. Consider five ways you can leave a legacy that will outlive you.

1. *Fear the Lord and obey Him.* Your legacy begins in your heart, in your relationship with God. On our first Christmas together, we gave to God the title deeds to our lives, to our marriage, to our family—to everything. Now, more than thirty-five years later, we marvel at all that He has accomplished in our lives and family.

2. *Recognize the world's needs, and respond with compassion and action.* You and your mate can leave a legacy by being committed to doing something positive about our world. Act with courage to reach out to those in need (see Matthew 9:36).

3. *Pray as a couple that God will use you to accomplish His purposes.* An Old Testament saint named Jabez asked God to bless him by giving him new turf and enlarging his sphere of influence, by keeping him from temptation, and by staying with him (1 Chron. 4:10). Our prayers ought to have the same kingdom focus.

4. *Help your mate be a better steward of his/her gifts and abilities.* Help him or her recognize how God already has used his or her gifts and abilities. Together, become actively involved in a local church that teaches God's Word faithfully and has a vision for the community.

5. *Ask God to give your children a sense of purpose, direction, and mission.* The challenge is to leave your children a biblical vision, not just an inheritance.

PONDER ON YOUR OWN

■ If you haven't done so yet, give God what is truly His: you! And your family!

DISCUSS WITH YOUR SPOUSE

■ How can you use your family to reach out in compassion to a hurting and needy world?

■ Ask each other how you could help one another to become better stewards of your gifts and abilities. How could you more effectively use these things for kingdom purposes?

STUDY WITH YOUR GROUP

■ What needs in your community could your group help to meet? How could you involve your families? Begin to plan at least one coordinated group outreach in the name of Christ.

3. Read Psalm 34:11

One of our most important missions is to teach our children what it means to fear God. John Witherspoon said, "It is only the fear of God that can deliver us from the fear of men."

If your child develops a reverential awe of God, then he or she will desire to please Him in every way. That will go a long way in overcoming the peer pressure and temptations this world is sure to bring! He or she will be more concerned with what God thinks than what anyone else thinks. So how can we train our children in the fear of God? We have found that effective training involves at least three parts.

First, parents need to clearly see the goal. They need to know what they are trying to achieve. Most parents have never written a mission statement for what they are trying to build into their children. It's no wonder so many parents feel like failures and don't really know if they've succeeded!

Second, effective training involves repetition. A Green Beret once told me, "As Green Berets, we train to learn what to do in every conceivable circumstance—over and over and over again. Then, in times of battle, we know what to do; it's just second nature to us." That is a picture of what parents should do. We train our children and instruct them in making good choices. And we do it over and over.

Finally, training involves accountability. One major mistake is giving our children too much freedom without appropriate oversight. This is especially true if a family has more than two children. We tend to overcontrol our first-born child and release the younger children prematurely. Avoid that trap through accountability.

PONDER ON YOUR OWN

How are you teaching your children what it means to "fear God"? What do you believe they are learning?

DISCUSS WITH YOUR SPOUSE

■ Ask your children what it means for them to "fear God." Don't correct them or define it for them; just ask them. What do their answers reveal to you?

■ If you have not yet together written out a mission statement for your children, begin to do so. What is on this mission statement? What seems most important to you? Why?

STUDY WITH YOUR GROUP

■ What strategies have you employed regarding repetition and accountability in regard to training your children in godliness? What has worked? What hasn't?

4. Read Psalm 78:1–8

What an awesome responsibility and privilege we have in these last days to be parents! Psalm 78 shows us the importance of leaving a godly heritage by making sure our children know of the wonderful works of God and His faithfulness to us.

And why are parents to teach their children what God has done? So that our children "may set their hope in God, and not forget the works of God, but keep His commandments" (78:7).

If anything makes a family distinctively Christian, it's that the mother and father remain committed to the Great Commandment, which is to love God with all their hearts, souls, minds, and strength (Mark 12:30), and to the Great Commission, which is, "Go therefore and make disciples of all the nations" (Matt. 28:19). When we build obedience to these two directives into our children's lives, we leave them with a great heritage indeed.

PONDER ON YOUR OWN

■ How have you tried to build into your children a desire to obey the Great Commandment? the Great Commission?

DISCUSS WITH YOUR SPOUSE

■ Why not use your next dinner together as a couple or a family to compile a list of what God has done in your lives and family? Keep the list active and live, adding to it on a regular basis.

STUDY WITH YOUR GROUP

■ Spend a good part of some evening telling each other about "the great works of God" that the Lord is doing in your own lives. How are these great works preparing you and your children for a lifetime of following Christ?

5. Read Galatians 6:9

Raising a family to the glory of God takes perseverance. As the great statesman Winston Churchill said, "Never give in, never give in, never, never, never, never—in nothing, great or small, large or petty—never give in except to convictions of honor and good sense."

Parenting is not a weekend project. We're talking years—the rest of your life, actually. Fortunately, adolescence has a time limit, but we'll never make it to the adult side of their maturation if we have to see immediate results.

Don't toss in the towel! If your parenting boat seems to be leaking like a sieve, keep bailing with one arm and row with the other. Perseverance is the indispensable parenting quality that helps you keep doing all the other important things—praying, training, and setting standards.

You *will* get tired. You *will* suffer. Your heart *will* ache. The ones for whom you are sacrificing—your children—will sometimes say and do things that hurt you. They do that because they are children, and "foolishness is bound up in the heart of a child" (Prov. 22:15). At times you may have to endure even a broken heart, but you must not lose heart, "for in due time we will reap if we do not grow weary" (Gal. 6:9 NASB).

PONDER ON YOUR OWN

■ In what area of your parenting experience do you most need perseverance right now? How can you gain the strength to persevere?

DISCUSS WITH YOUR SPOUSE

■ Ask each other what you can do to better help each other endure hard times with your children. What most drives you nuts with your kids? How can your spouse help?

■ In what areas of your parenting do you most feel the urge to "give in" right now? How can you encourage and equip the other to persevere instead?

STUDY WITH YOUR GROUP

▨ Sometimes a word or a gesture from an "outsider" can have a more positive, immediate effect on a son or daughter than the same thing coming from a parent. Brainstorm some ways you might become that helpful "outsider" for others in your group, and then make a plan to see it happen.

6. Read Deuteronomy 5:9

Deuteronomy 5:9 sends cold shivers down the spines of some believers: "I . . . am a jealous God, visiting the iniquity of the fathers upon the children to the third and fourth generations of those who hate me."

What do you think this warning means? Is God trying to deliberately ruin the next generation? Why would God set up a system that inflicts one generation's flaws on three or four others?

I have a hunch that God is trying to tell us that the way we live is of supreme importance. Possibly, He's using a warning of future judgment on our descendants to keep us on the straight and narrow today.

Whether you like it or not, your children are becoming just like you. Their little eyes are watching to see how you relate to your mate, how you pray, how you walk with Christ every day. They hear your words and subconsciously mimic your attitudes, actions, and even your mannerisms.

And as time goes by, you'll find they've inherited some of the same tendencies toward sin that you learned from your parents. And the time to stop that behavior is *now*.

PONDER ON YOUR OWN

■ What do you think about the statement, "Whether you like it or not, your children are becoming just like you"? If this is true, do you see that as a good or a bad thing? Why?

DISCUSS WITH YOUR SPOUSE

■ Read Deuteronomy 5:9 together and discuss its meaning. What does this verse have to say about the way you are raising your children?

■ Read Jesus' words in Luke 6:40. What does this verse have to say about the way you are raising your children? What feeling, if any, does it prompt within you?

STUDY WITH YOUR GROUP

■ How have you noticed your children becoming just like you? What in their words, actions, and attitudes has caused you to take notice? What funny incidents have occurred? What more sobering incidents have occurred? What, if anything, does this encourage you to start (or stop) doing with your children?

7. Read Acts 5:1–11

If Ananias and Sapphira had children, what sort of heritage do you think this foolish couple left to their orphans? Their sad story makes me wonder—if we could see how our sin affected our descendants, would it make a difference in the way we live today?

One of our ministry staff members is committed to breaking the chains of his past. When speaking to individuals considering vocational Christian ministry, he always says, "I grew up in a broken home, and I don't want to end up like my father. He lived his life for himself, and in the end, at his funeral, only ten people showed up. I want a *packed* funeral, full of lives my life has impacted. I want to leave a legacy that will outlast me."

I'll be honest with you. The thought of my kids falling prey to the sin in the same areas that I feel tempted has bolstered my obedience to God. I'm reminded of the piercing statement by C. H. Spurgeon: "Sin would have fewer takers if its consequences occurred immediately."

In the case of Ananias and Sapphira, the consequences *did* occur immediately. But what of the consequences to the next generation? For your own spiritual health, and for the sake of your children, make a fresh commitment to holiness in your life today.

PONDER ON YOUR OWN

What patterns of sin in your life may you need to confess to God and turn from?

DISCUSS WITH YOUR SPOUSE

What changes might be required in your marriage to break any "chains" from your past?

■ Discuss a time when you saw the blessing of God on your marriage and family, which you knew came because of your obedience.

STUDY WITH YOUR GROUP

■ What problems that plague other couples and families most worry you? How can obedience to the lordship of Christ enable you to avoid, or at least greatly reduce, those problems?

8. Read Joshua 4

The fourth chapter of Joshua records one of the most significant events in the history of Israel. It also gives us a potent example to follow and one of the most powerful spiritual principles in the Bible.

To commemorate Israel's crossing of the Jordan River, the Lord told His people to erect a monument of twelve stones, one stone for each tribe. Those dozen stones were meant to become a spiritual reminder to future generations about God's guidance and provision for His people.

Most of us won't be crossing the Jordan anytime soon, but we can still follow the example of the ancient Israelites. We are wise if we find creative ways, as couples and families, to commemorate landmarks in our lives—events such as significant birthdays, graduations, weddings, commitments we've made to the Lord individually and as families, or an instance in which God has clearly done something great in us or for us.

PONDER ON YOUR OWN

▨ Besides the day you accepted Christ, the day you got married, or the day your child was born, what event has had the most profound effect on your spiritual life? How have you recorded some memory of this event for future reference?

DISCUSS WITH YOUR SPOUSE

▨ Acquire a family Bible or find another visible means of collecting spiritual "memorial stones" and begin recording significant family events, especially for the dull, drab days when doubt and fear cloud your soul.

▨ In the past year, how have you seen God guide you and provide for your family in a unique way? How can you commemorate these things?

STUDY WITH YOUR GROUP

▨ What "memorial stones" have you set up for your family? What do they commemorate? How have you used them in the spiritual development of your children?

9. Read Psalm 127:3–5

In Psalm 127:4, God compares children to "arrows in the hand of a warrior." Arrows are not designed to stay in the quiver. They are created for flight, to rush toward God's target. They're meant for battle. And from the time you bring them home from the hospital, those little arrows must be shaped, sharpened, and honed for God's intended purpose.

Every archer worth his salt can tell you there is pain in launching an arrow. As the archer lets go, his left forearm can be painfully stung with the slap of the string. The same is true of a parent's heart. While the arrow is enjoying the flight he was made for, the parent's heart feels the sting of the release.

Releasing is also scary. It's scary because, as has been well said, a child is a parent's heart walking around outside his body. Will he fly straight? Will she get blown off course? Will they fall short of God's intended destination for their lives?

You'll never know if you don't release them. You'll never know what God has intended specifically for each one. In fact, they'll never grow up at all if you keep them safe in your quiver, away from the battlefield.

We've launched six, and trust me, it got tougher to let go with each arrow. But we've learned that we must let go if our children are to fly toward the target that God has set up just for them.

PONDER ON YOUR OWN

- What "targets" do you think God may have in mind for your child or children? What makes you think of these targets? How can you begin now to prepare your children for "flight"?

DISCUSS WITH YOUR SPOUSE

- What makes you feel most anxious about letting your arrows fly? Why?

What balance do you try to achieve in your children's lives between safety and necessary risk? How are you teaching your kids to "go for it" for God?

STUDY WITH YOUR GROUP

Have any of you already "launched an arrow"? If so, describe the experience. What was hard about it? What was exhilarating? What would you do the same? What would you do differently? How can all of you, regardless of where your children are in the process, resist the urge to pull that arrow back and into the quiver where it's safe?

10. Read 2 Samuel 7:14–16

If you're a mother or father, one of your top concerns must be to focus on the kind of legacy you are leaving behind. Are you diligently working to raise your children to love and fear God and walk with Him?

Speaking through the prophet Nathan, God gave David an amazing word picture of his legacy. The Lord said of David's son Solomon, "I will be his Father, and he shall be My son . . . your house and your kingdom shall be established forever before you. Your throne shall be established forever" (7:14, 16).

Our culture stands in desperate need of reformation, and that can happen only when godly individuals begin doing what they must do to leave behind a godly legacy. This has to start with each of us determining what type of legacy we want to pass on to our children.

How will your children remember you? Will they remember you as a man or woman preoccupied with the things of this world? Or will they recall their parents as committed children of God who modeled a life-changing faith in Jesus Christ?

Legacies are comprised of the choices we make. Someone has said, "The doors of opportunity swing on the little hinges of obedience." If you could look ahead in time twenty, thirty, even forty years, *how will your children remember you?*

PONDER ON YOUR OWN

■ What choices are you making today, this week, or in the near future that may affect your legacy? How does pondering this question affect the decisions you will make?

DISCUSS WITH YOUR SPOUSE

■ Discuss the question, "If you could look ahead in time twenty, thirty, even forty years, *how will your children remember you?*" How would you *want* them to remember you? What needs to happen in order for them to remember you in this way?

STUDY WITH YOUR GROUP

■ Discuss the statement, "The doors of opportunity swing on the little hinges of obedience." What does it mean? Do you agree with it? Why or why not? If true, what significance does it have for your own parenting and families?

■ What type of legacy do you want to pass on to your children? How do you plan to build such a legacy? How can others help you build that kind of legacy?

EPILOGUE

You Get What You Plant

The laws of nature teach us that you never harvest one thing after you've planted something else. You don't get watermelons by planting cucumbers.

Marriage works the same way—we never get out of marriage what we do not put into it. One man confessed to me, "At work I concentrate on winning, and as a result, I am a winner. At home, however, I concentrate on just getting by."

No wonder he is losing. The seed he planted—neglect—will produce in kind.

Americans normally think of themselves as winners. We are used to winning, but too many times, in the wrong places. As a result, we end up losing in the important places, such as at home. The late Vance Havner once said, "Americans know the price of everything, but the value of nothing."

You and I must master the ageless art of leadership and apply it to our families. If we ever hope to win at home, then we must consider what kind of harvest we want in the end. If we plant seeds of commitment to Christ and to one another, along with seeds of forgiveness and respect, then we can look forward to the day when God will grant us a great harvest.

We'd like to end this study by suggesting ten "seeds" for you to plant, bound to yield (in time!) a delightful and rich harvest. We have Dr. Willard Harley Jr. and his excellent book *His Needs, Her Needs* to thank for the potting proposals:

Top Five Ways for a Man to Please His Wife

1. Have a strong commitment to your family; make it a priority.

2. Provide security: emotional, financial, personal protection, etc.

3. Be willing to be her partner, to share life with her in honest, open relationship.

4. Talk with her in complete sentences; take time to discuss subjects with her.

5. Provide nonsexual affection: hugging, touching, tenderness, closeness that doesn't demand a sexual response.

Top Five Ways for a Woman to Please Her Husband

1. Show your mate admiration and respect through verbal praise.

2. Provide domestic support—help to keep the home in order.

3. Be attractive; he wants to be proud of you.

4. Offer recreational companionship.

5. Help him to pleasure you through an exciting, satisfying sexual union.[1]

Week Two

1. Dave Roever. *Welcome Home Davey* (Nashville: W Publishing Group, 1986).

Week Four

1. William Barclay. *New Daily Study Bible: The Letter to the Corinthians* (Kentucky: Westminster John Knox Press, 2002).
2. John G. Alvidsen. *Rocky.* United Artists, 1976.

Week Five

1. Ney Bailey. *Faith Is Not a Feeling* (Colorado Springs: Waterbrook, 2002).

Week Six

1. Herbert Agar. *A Time for Greatness* (Boston: Little, Brown and Company, 1942).
2. William Manchester. *The Last Lion* (New York: Little, Brown and Company, 1983).

Week Seven

1. Neil Postman. *The Disappearance of Childhood* (New York: Vintage/Random House, 1994).

Epilogue

1. Dr. Willard Harley, Jr. *His Needs, Her Needs* (Grand Rapids: Revell, 2005).